A Pragmatic Approach to English Language Teaching and Production

Edited by

Lala U. Takeda
Megumi Okugiri

KAZAMA SHOBO

Contents

Acknowledgements ·· 1

Introduction ···························· *Lala U. Takeda and Megumi Okugiri* 3

Part 1 Learning Pragmatics in a Studying Abroad Context

Effects of Speech Act on Learners' Pragmatic Development in a Study
    Abroad Context ··· *Naoko Osuka* 9
Investigating the Effects of Short-Term Study Abroad on the Listenership
    of Japanese EFL University Students
        ···*Pino Cutrone and Keisuke Imamura* 33

Part 2 Teaching and Production of Pragmatics in Academic Writing:
        Seeking the Relation to Speaking

Differences in the Quality of Interaction between Spoken and Written
    Communication ··· *Misa Fujio* 63
Overuse of "Reason": Effect of L1 Transfer on L2 English and Japanese
    Writing ··· *Megumi Okugiri* 83
Constructive Criticism in Talk-in-Interaction: Experienced Japanese EFL
    Learners' Peer-Feedback Sessions on English Essays
        ···*Ivan B. Brown and Ayaka Takeuchi* 109

Part 3   The Acquisition of Pragmatics Through Interaction and Teaching

Exploring Implicit and Explicit Teaching Methods in EFL Education:
   A Cross-Genre Analysis of Topic Management Through Overlaps
   .... *Lala U. Takeda*   143
From Needs Analysis to Emergent Pragmatic Competence:
   A Longitudinal Micro-Analytic Study of Learner Talk in Japanese EFL
   University Classes .... *John Campbell-Larsen*   169
The Use of Spontaneous Gesture as a Multimodal Interactional Strategy
   in English as a Lingua Franca Interactions: The Case of Non-
   Understanding Sequences .... *Hiroki Hanamoto*   199

List of Editors and Contributors

Editors

Lala U. Takeda	Tokyo Denki University
Megumi Okugiri	University of the Sacred Heart

Contributors

Ivan B. Brown	Joetsu University of Education
John Campbell-Larsen	Kyoto Women's University
Pino Cutrone	Nagasaki University
Misa Fujio	Toyo University
Hiroki Hanamoto	Tokyo Denki University
Keisuke Imamura	Tokyo Medical and Dental University
Naoko Osuka	Meiji University
Ayaka Takeuchi	Shimodate Daiichi High School

(Alphabetical order)

Acknowledgements

Our gratitude is especially given to Professor Paul Rossiter, Dr. Troy McConachy, Dr. David Allen and Travis Garcia for their helpful comments and insightful suggestion on our proposal as well as for their warm support in all stages of the production of this volume. We also would like to thank Dennis Harmon, Ben McDonough, Ivan B. Brown, and Junko Kosaki on our workshop at JACET in 2017 through their lively discussion and valuable comments. We would like to show sincere gratitude to Professor Tom Gally, Dr. Shin'ichiro Ishikawa, Dr. Yuko Itatsu, and Dr. Yukiko Mishina for their earlier support to publish this book. As editors, we gratefully acknowledge all the contributors to this collection for their sincere and kind cooperation on every phase of this book publishing. Lastly, we are deeply indebted to Keiko Kazama of Kazama Shobo for her encouragement and careful treatment of our manuscripts. This publication was supported by JSPS KAKENHI Grant Number 19HP5063.

Introduction

Lala U. Takeda and Megumi Okugiri

This volume is based on a thought-provoking symposium entitled "Contributions to English language teaching from a pragmatic approach: A discussion on English as a foreign language (EFL) textbook materials and teaching methods for conversation and writing" at the Japan Association of College English Teachers (JACET) 56th International Convention (2017, Tokyo). It elucidated the significance of learners' pragmatic competence and improvement with regard to teaching and production, and its success encouraged us to disseminate the most contemporary and relevant research on teaching and production in the speaking and writing domains without being confined to the papers presented at the symposium.

The aim of this book is to present new perspectives on the teaching and production of speaking and writing, in terms of pragmatics, with regard to second language (L2) learners. In the process of acquisition, L2 learners show a variety of pragmatic and communication strategies toward different interlocutors or readers. This volume will show that teaching pragmatics makes L2 learners aware of the changes in attitude toward communication. There has been a growing need for empirical and theoretical studies focused on the effect of study-abroad experience as well as the teaching and production of speaking and writing, especially concerning context-dependent, moment-to-moment communicative behaviors. This book will address this need by focusing on English as a Foreign Language (EFL) learners from Japan. It will provide readers with a comprehensive understanding of the differences and similarities in production between L2 and L1, particularly speaking and writing and the pragmatics. Understanding these phenomena will help English language instructors to cultivate EFL learners' perception and appreciation of differences not only in language but also in the culture of L2, which facilitate their effective application of their newly acquired second language in real-world communication.

The book contains eight latest developments in L2 acquisition area, organized into three parts. Part 1 (Learning Pragmatics in a Studying Abroad Context) focuses on the influence of study-abroad experience on L2 pragmatic ability. The contributors provide a comparison between their findings and those of previous studies on context-appropriate behaviors.

Part 2 (Teaching and Production of Pragmatics in Academic Writing: Seeking the Relation to Speaking) is based on the presence of unique features in L2 writing production. This part reveals genre-specific functions and communication strategies in L2 essay writing, and it focuses on the relationship between speaking and writing from interactive aspect in written communication and peer-feedback sessions for English essays so as to serve to bridge the research on writing and speaking by L2 learners.

Part 3 (The Acquisition of Pragmatics Through Interaction and Teaching) discusses teaching pedagogy in speaking and ways to ameliorate L2 learners' awareness of context-dependency and creativity in co-constructing meaning within an interaction.

This book will contribute to future researchers in the following areas: second language acquisition, conversation analysis in L2 settings, interactional sociolinguistics, interlanguage pragmatics, intercultural (pragmatic) competence, L2 learner motivation, L2 learners' individual differences, L1 transfer, L2 classroom research, L2 academic writing, cognitive linguistics, English as a Lingua Franca (ELF), and L2 education in Asian countries. It will also serve the needs of EFL language teachers.

Part 1: Learning Pragmatics in a Studying Abroad Context

Effects of Speech Act on Learners' Pragmatic Development in a Study Abroad Context

Naoko Osuka

Abstract

Few studies have empirically examined the possibility that the type of speech acts, such as requests, apologies, and refusals, may affect L2 learners' pragmatic development. The present study investigates the effects of speech acts on learners' pragmatic development, by examining the changes of the appropriateness of their performance through study abroad experiences. Twenty-two study abroad students performed a multimedia elicitation task (MET), which included three speech acts, before and after studying abroad. Seven native speakers evaluated the appropriateness of their utterances. The comparison between the appropriateness scores before and after studying abroad revealed that expressing gratitude is easier for L2 learners to develop than requesting and refusing in a study abroad context. It is suggested that the abundant exposure, the rather simple structure, and the acquisition of some versatile pragmatic routines, such as 'Thank you so much' and 'I (really) appreciate', could facilitate their development in expressing gratitude. On the other hand, requesting could be difficult for learners because there are many politeness levels with various conventional expressions in requests. Refusing might be the most difficult speech act to develop in a study abroad context because of the complex structure and the lack of versatile pragmatic routines.

Keywords: pragmatic development, speech acts, study abroad, pragmatic routines

Introduction

In recent years there have been an increasing number of longitudinal studies that investigate L2 learners' pragmatic development in a study abroad context. These previous studies suggest that various factors could affect L2 learners' pragmatic development, including length of stay (e.g., Blum-Kulka & Olthtain, 1986; Félix-Brasdefer, 2004), intensity of interaction (e.g., Barodvi-Harlig & Bastos, 2011; Kasper & Rose, 2002) and proficiency (e.g. Barodvi-Harlig & Dörnyei, 1998). Some previous studies have also pointed to the possibility that the type of speech acts, such as requests, apologies, and refusals, may affect L2 learners' pragmatic development. For example, Kasper and Schmidt (1996) state that speech acts with higher complexity, such as refusals, tend to be late in successful production. However, there have been few studies which empirically examined whether speech acts affect learners' pragmatic development by comparing the same learners' development data in different speech acts.

The current study is a part of a larger one which investigates Japanese learners' pragmatic development in a study abroad context in the realization of three speech acts: requests, refusals, and expressing gratitude. This paper focuses on the effects of speech acts on learners' pragmatic development by examining the appropriateness of their performance.

Previous Studies

It seems that a study abroad environment is advantageous for learners' pragmatic development because they have abundant input and output opportunities to use their target language on a daily basis during their sojourn. Therefore, they are assumed to make more gains than their counterparts who remain studying in their home country. This assumption has been examined by focusing on different speech acts using a longitudinal design. Many studies reported positive effects of study abroad experiences on learners' pragmatic development (e.g., Barron, 2003; Matsumura, 2001, 2003; Schauer, 2009; Shiverly, 2011) whereas some did not support this claim (e.g. Battaler, 2010). However, there have been only a limited number of studies which investigated the same L2 learners' pragmatic development in different speech acts at the same time.

Hoffman-Hicks (2000) investigated the pragmatic development by 14 American students who studied French in France for 16 months, in their realization of the speech acts of greeting, leave-taking, and compliments. A production questionnaire was used to elicit data three times during the period. The data were compared with those of 10 students who studied in their home country and those of 14 French native speakers. The analysis revealed that the learners showed pragmatic development over time, but that the development was slight and limited. It was confirmed, however, that they made gains from study abroad experiences because the control group did not demonstrate even slight development. Furthermore, the learners demonstrated greater gains in greeting and leave-taking than in compliments. This suggests that some speech acts are easier to acquire than others.

In Barron's (2003) study, 33 Irish learners of German studied in Germany for 10 months. Production questionnaires and retrospective interviews were used to collect data in realization of requests, offers, and refusals of offers. The data collection was conducted three times: before coming to Germany, in the middle of the sojourn, and toward the end of it. The elicited data were compared with those of 34 German native speakers and 53 Irish native speakers. The results revealed that the learners demonstrated development to some extent toward the target norms, such as increased use of syntactic and lexical/phrasal downgraders in requesting and less complex offer-refusal sequences. However, Barron found that some developments differed from the target norms. Furthermore, the results showed that changes were slower in refusals compared with those in requests and offers.

Cohen and Shively (2007) investigated L2 learners' acquisition of requests and apologies. Participants were 86 American university students who studied in a Spanish- or a French-speaking country for one semester. They were divided into an experimental group that received a curricular intervention on language and culture strategies and a control group that did not receive this assistance. The learners' performances were rated by Spanish and French native speakers. The results revealed that the combined experimental and control groups demonstrated significant improvement in their performance of speech acts of requests and apologies. However, there were no significant differences between the experimental and control groups probably because of insufficient intervention. Although the authors do not directly describe the developmental differences between the participants' request and apology performances, the presented data suggest that the participants showed more development in requests than in apologies. In requests, significant change occurred at the 1% or 0.1% level in four out of five vignettes, while in apologies, they occurred only in two out of five vignettes. When calculating the mean rating score of each speech act performance, based on the figures displayed in the table (Table 1 on p. 200), the participants' total mean scores of requests were slightly lower than those of apologies in the pre-test (requests: 17.00; apologies: 17.08); however, in the post-test, the scores of requests were higher than those of apologies (requests: 18.88; apologies: 18.35).

Overall, these previous studies suggest that pragmatic development could be affected by the type of speech acts in a study abroad context. Some speech acts may be easier to perform or develop in contrast to others that could be more difficult and take more time to develop. However, as the number of previous studies which directly compared the same learners' development using different speech acts is limited, further investigation of a greater variety of learners and speech acts is necessary. Thus, the research questions of the current study are:

1) Are some speech acts easier for L2 learners to *perform* than other speech acts?
2) Are some speech acts easier for L2 learners to *develop in a study abroad context* than other speech acts?

Method

Participants

Twenty-two Japanese college students, 7 males and 15 females, who studied in the United States for one semester (henceforth SA students) participated in this study. They are students of the same university in Tokyo, aged 19 to 21 years. At the beginning of the research, none of them had stayed abroad for more than one month. Their mean score of the TOEFL iBT test was 66.77 (SD: 4.14). The SA students studied for four to six months in various places in the U.S., including New York, Oregon, Alabama, Indiana, and Florida. They lived in dormitories during their sojourn in the U.S., with the exception of one student who stayed with an American family.

Twenty Japanese college students (henceforth AH students) who studied in their home country, 6 males and 14 females, also participated in this study as a control group. They are undergraduates, with ages ranging from 19 to 21 years. Similarly they did not have any experience of staying abroad for more than one month. Their TOEFL iBT scores ranged from 53 to 77, and the mean score was 67.65 (SD: 6.73). There was no significant difference between the SA and AH groups' TOEFL iBT scores at the beginning of the research.

Twenty-two American college students, 9 males and 13 females, (henceforth NE students) participated in this study to provide baseline data. All the NE students are undergraduate students.

Instrument

The data were elicited through a multimedia elicitation task (henceforth MET). The MET, which was originally developed by Schauer (2004), is a computer-based data elicitation tool. It is a kind of oral DCT (Discourse Completion Task) with a one-turn format. Participants look at a photograph on a computer screen and listen to an audio script which describes a situation. Then they are asked to say what they would say if they were in the same situation. Their utterances are automatically recorded.

The MET has some advantages compared with other data collection methods. First, the MET has better comparability and practicality than role plays, in that it provides exactly the same input by a computer, not by real interlocutors. Compared with written DCTs, the MET can offer more realistic context, by providing visual/audio input and an interactive format. Another advantage is that it elicits oral data, which contain more features of naturally occurring talk than written data (Schauer, 2009). Finally, unlike written DCTs, the MET does not allow participants to have planning time; thus, the MET enables the researcher to examine learners' implicit knowledge, rather than explicit knowledge.

On the other hand, there are also disadvantages with the MET, including lack of interaction and consequences. As Félix-Brasdefer (2010) points out, "[It] cannot capture the dynamics of social (face-to-face) interaction that allow us to examine speech act sequences across multiple turns as role plays do." (p. 47)

The MET used for the present study was developed by the author in order to investigate the pragmatic development of Japanese learners of English in their realization of speech acts of requests, refusals, and expressing gratitude. It has 24 scenarios: The first eight scenarios focus on requests, the second set of eight targets refusals, and the remaining set of eight focuses on expressing gratitude. Table 1 displays brief descriptions of each scenario.

The three types of speech acts were chosen because they differ from each other in their nature. While requesting is a speech act initiated by the speaker, refusing and expressing gratitude are speech acts that respond to another speech act or an act performed by an interlocutor. From a face-saving perspective, requesting and refusing are essentially face-threatening

Table 1
Brief descriptions of scenarios

Sit.	Brief description
Requests	
1	Asking a friend to let you use her pen. [*pen 1*]
2	Asking a friend for the time [*time*]
3	Asking a friend to let you copy her lecture notes [*notes*]
4	Asking a friend to be interviewed for your research [*interview 1*]
5	Asking a teacher to turn on the air conditioner [*AC*]
6	Asking a teacher to speak louder [*louder*]
7	Asking a teacher to write a recommendation letter [*letter 1*]
8	Asking a teacher for an extension of a deadline [*deadline*]
Refusals	
9	Refusing a snack offered by a friend [*snack*]
10	Refusing a student's request to sit next to you [*seat*]
11	Refusing a friend's invitation to a small party [*party*]
12	Refusing a student's suggestion to join a drama group [*drama*]
13	Refusing coffee offered by a teacher [*coffee*]
14	Refusing a teacher's suggestion to join a study group [*study group*]
15	Refusing a teacher's request to help at a school event [*school event*]
16	Refusing a teacher's invitation to a barbecue party [*barbecue*]
Expressing gratitude	
17	Thanking a friend for lending you $1 [*money*]
18	Thanking a friend for picking up your pen [*pen 2*]
19	Thanking a friend for giving you a souvenir [*souvenir*]
20	Thanking a student for helping with your research [*interview 2*]
21	Thanking a teacher for giving you a handout [*handout*]
22	Thanking a teacher for giving you information about a summer study program [*information*]
23	Thanking a teacher for writing a recommendation letter for you [*letter 2*]
24	Thanking a teacher for lending you a book [*book*]

Note: Sit. =Situation

acts (Brown & Levinson, 1987), whereas expressing gratitude is a face-enhancing act for the hearer (Leech, 2014).

There are two variables incorporated in the study: social status and the size of imposition. For the study of refusals, the types of the preceding speech acts (i.e., offer, request, invitation, and suggestion) are also considered as the variables.

Some of the scenarios were taken from previous research and modified for this study (Beebe, Takahashi & Uliss-Weltz, 1990; Blum-Kulka, House & Kasper, 1989; Clankie, 1993; Eisenstein & Bodman, 1993; Félix-Brasdefer, 2004; Nakai, 2004; Rose & Ono, 1995; Sasaki, 1998; Schauer, 2009). The remaining scenarios were developed by the author based on suggestions from students who had a study abroad experience and the author's own experience. All the scenarios were checked by four native English speakers to ensure that they reflect typical situations that participants would likely encounter in a study abroad context. (See Osuka (2017) for the complete scenarios).

The SA students conducted the MET twice, before and after their study abroad experience. The collected data were analyzed in terms of their use of pragmatic strategies, internal/external modification, and pragmatic routines. Furthermore, an appropriateness assessment by native speakers was conducted.

Data analysis

To investigate the participants' pragmatic development from a holistic perspective, an appropriateness assessment by native speakers was conducted. Native speaking raters were six Americans and one Canadian who had recently come to Japan. They were all female undergraduates. As the amount of data was large, the raters were divided into two groups: Groups A and B. Four raters (Group A) assessed Situations 1-4, 9-12, and 17-20. Three raters (Group B) assessed Situations 5-8, 13-16, and 21-24.

There was a prior training session for all the raters together before they started rating. In the training session, the researcher explained the purpose of the research and the procedure of the appropriateness assessment, including the rating criteria and guidelines. They were also asked to rate the imposition of each situation using a 7-point Lickert scale. The results are presented in Tables 3 and 4. Finally, the session included practice and discussion using some examples.

With regard to the rating criteria, following Taguchi's (2011a) definition of appropriateness as "the ability to perform speech acts at the proper level of

Table 2
Appropriateness rating scale

Ratings	Descriptions
5 Excellent	Almost perfectly appropriate and effective on the levels of directness, politeness and formality.
4 Good	Not perfect but adequately appropriate on the levels of directness, politeness and formality. Expressions are a little off from native-like but pretty good.
3 Fair	Somewhat appropriate on the levels of directness, politeness and formality. Expressions are more direct or indirect than the situation requires.
2 Poor	Clearly inappropriate. Expressions sound almost rude/too demanding or unnaturally polite.
1 Very poor	The utterance is impossible to understand.

politeness, directness, and formality in the given situations" (p. 273), a 5-point Likert scale, ranging from 1 (Very poor) to 5 (Excellent) was used. Taguchi's (2011b, p. 459) rating scale was modified for the study. Table 2 presents the appropriateness rating scale for the current study. The raters were asked to rate each response of the SA and the AH students, both pre- and post-study abroad, according to the rating criteria. They were instructed to disregard minor grammatical mistakes if these did not hinder communication, as the focus of the study was on situational appropriateness. To avoid causing bias in assessment, all the data were randomly mixed before being sent to the raters. Thus, the raters did not know who had produced each response.

Judgements of pragmatic appropriateness are complicated, largely due to the nature of pragmatics. Taguchi (2011b) reports that raters can vary greatly "in their perceptions and interpretations of appropriateness, politeness, and formality in pragmatic performance because they come from cultures that have very different community norms for social interaction and communicative events" (p. 468). The inter-rater reliabilities (Cronbach alpha) of the current study were 0.802 for Group A and 0.749 for Group B. Considering the nature of pragmatics, these inter-rater reliabilities were considered sufficient.

Results

Table 3 presents the SA group's mean scores for the appropriateness assessment in all three speech acts. Table 4 presents those of the AH group.

A comparison of the overall mean scores of the three speech acts in the SA group reveals that the mean score is the highest in expressing gratitude (pre: 3.83; post: 4.08), the second highest in refusals (pre: 3.60; post:

Table 3

Comparison of the SA group's mean scores between pre- and post-study abroad (n=22)

Situations	Pre Mean	SD	Post Mean	SD	p-value (df)		Status	Imposition	Preceding speech act
Requests									
1. pen 1	4.36	0.93	4.27	0.73	.694	(21)	equal	1.86	
2. time	3.88	1.24	3.72	0.94	.586	(21)	equal	1.86	
3. notes	3.55	1.08	3.94	1.04	.090†	(21)	equal	4.00	
4. interview1	3.26	1.17	3.64	0.94	.111	(21)	equal	5.00	
5. AC	3.27	1.02	3.70	1.11	.159	(21)	higher	3.71	
6. louder	2.85	0.87	3.68	0.73	.000***	(21)	higher	3.57	
7. letter 1	3.14	0.79	3.12	0.43	.941	(21)	higher	4.86	
8. deadline	2.80	0.75	3.08	0.80	.276	(21)	higher	6.14	
Overall mean of requests	3.39	1.01	3.64	0.83	.004**	(175)		3.88	
Refusals									
9. snack	4.13	0.94	4.38	0.61	.287	(21)	equal	1.43	offer
10. seat	3.99	0.75	4.16	0.74	.463	(21)	equal	4.57	request
11. party	4.23	0.48	4.36	0.47	.229	(21)	equal	2.71	invitation
12. drama	3.89	0.61	3.91	0.83	.918	(21)	equal	1.86	suggestion
13. coffee	3.36	1.27	3.74	1.05	.196	(21)	higher	2.00	offer
14. study group	2.33	0.78	2.73	0.79	.085†	(21)	higher	3.43	suggestion
15. school event	3.48	0.75	3.53	0.66	.781	(21)	higher	4.57	request
16. barbecue	3.36	0.76	3.59	0.61	.249	(21)	higher	2.86	invitation
Overall mean of refusals	3.60	0.99	3.80	0.88	.006**	(175)		2.93	
Expressing gratitude									
17. money	4.00	1.02	4.31	0.67	.067†	(21)	equal	3.00	
18. pen 2	4.48	0.76	4.83	0.43	.037*	(21)	equal	1.71	
19. souvenir	4.36	0.73	4.64	0.61	.026*	(21)	equal	5.43	
20. interview 2	4.20	0.87	4.43	0.87	.040*	(21)	equal	5.57	
21. handout	3.57	1.20	3.91	0.84	.164	(21)	higher	3.29	
22. information	3.56	1.02	3.62	0.92	.787	(21)	higher	4.86	
23. letter 2	3.11	0.88	3.47	0.12	.067†	(21)	higher	6.57	
24. book	3.33	0.81	3.47	1.01	.368	(21)	higher	5.00	
Overall mean of expressing gratitude	3.83	0.85	4.08	0.75	.000***	(175)		4.43	

Note: †$p<.10$ *$p<.05$ **$p<.01$ ***$p<.001$

Table 4
Comparison of the AH group's mean scores between pre- and post-tests (n=20)

Situations	Pre Mean	Pre SD	Post Mean	Post SD	p-value	(df)	Status	Imposition	Preceding speech act
Requests									
1. pen 1	4.49	1.43	4.45	1.60	.834	(19)	equal	1.86	
2. time	3.85	1.20	3.84	0.90	.944	(19)	equal	1.86	
3. notes	3.70	0.98	3.53	0.78	.327	(19)	equal	4.00	
4. interview1	3.56	0.98	3.23	0.94	.111	(19)	equal	5.00	
5. AC	3.13	0.95	3.33	1.14	.453	(19)	higher	3.71	
6. louder	2.90	0.92	2.97	0.93	.787	(19)	higher	3.57	
7. letter 1	2.45	0.79	2.98	0.43	.015*	(19)	higher	4.86	
8. deadline	2.73	0.53	2.55	0.79	.322	(19)	higher	6.14	
Overall mean of requests	3.35	1.07	3.36	1.02	.944	(159)		3.88	
Refusals									
9. snack	3.91	0.82	4.19	0.93	.231	(19)	equal	1.43	offer
10. seat	3.74	1.02	4.03	0.66	.235	(19)	equal	4.57	request
11. party	4.20	0.64	4.18	0.49	.890	(19)	equal	2.71	invitation
12. drama	3.95	0.46	4.14	0.75	.218	(19)	equal	1.86	suggestion
13. coffee	3.22	0.96	3.22	1.17	1.000	(19)	higher	2.00	offer
14. study group	2.30	0.51	2.32	0.66	.919	(19)	higher	3.43	suggestion
15. school event	3.25	0.62	3.30	0.88	.845	(19)	higher	4.57	request
16. barbecue	3.07	0.85	3.38	0.41	.185	(19)	higher	2.86	invitation
Overall mean of refusals	3.45	0.94	3.59	0.98	.083†	(159)		2.93	
Expressing gratitude									
17. money	3.96	0.56	3.88	0.82	.660	(19)	equal	3.00	
18. pen 2	4.58	0.66	4.31	0.70	.190	(19)	equal	1.71	
19. souvenir	4.43	0.32	4.30	0.57	.415	(19)	equal	5.43	
20. interview 2	4.13	0.73	4.06	0.67	.792	(19)	equal	5.57	
21. handout	3.75	1.15	3.63	0.80	.661	(19)	higher	3.29	
22. information	3.43	0.77	3.68	0.93	.383	(19)	higher	4.86	
23. letter 2	3.18	0.63	3.38	0.74	.390	(19)	higher	6.57	
24. book	3.38	0.70	3.33	0.82	.799	(19)	higher	5.00	
Overall mean of expressing gratitude	3.85	0.85	3.82	0.83	.681	(159)		4.43	

Note: †p<.10 *p<.05

3.80), and the lowest in requests (pre: 3.39; post: 3.64) both before and after the study abroad. The results of paired t-tests of the SA group's overall mean scores show that, before studying abroad, there are significant differences between the mean scores of expressing gratitude and those of the other speech acts (expressing gratitude vs. refusals: $p=.020$; expressing gratitude vs. requests: $p<.001$). There is a marginally significant difference between requests and refusals ($p=.052$). The results are similar in the post-tests. After studying abroad, the differences are significant between expressing gratitude and the other speech acts (expressing gratitude vs. refusals: $p=.001$; expressing gratitude vs. requests: $p<.001$). There is a marginally significant difference between requests and refusals ($p=.084$). The rank order of the overall mean scores of the three speech acts is the same in the AH group both in the pre- and post-tests. These results could suggest that expressing gratitude is easier to perform for L2 learners than the other two speech acts, and that requests could be the most difficult among the three speech acts.

When comparing the SA group's overall mean scores for each speech act before and after studying abroad by using two-tailed, paired-sample t-tests, there is a significant increase in all the three speech acts. In requests, the overall mean score increased from 3.39 to 3.64 at the 1% level ($p=.004$). Similarly, in refusals, the mean score increased from 3.60 to 3.80 at the 1% level ($p=.006$). In expressing gratitude, the increase was at the 0.1% level: from 3.83 to 4.08 ($p<.001$). On the other hand, in the AH group, there is no significant difference between the overall mean scores in the pre-test and those of the post-test in any of the three speech acts. The different results between the SA and AH groups could provide evidence for the positive effects of studying abroad experiences on L2 learners' pragmatic development in the three types of speech acts.

A closer examination reveals that there are some differences in the SA group's development among the three speech acts. In requests, the increase of mean scores in the SA group is statistically significant in one (Situation 6) out of eight situations, and marginally significant in one situation (Situation 3). In refusals, although the overall mean scores indicate a significant increase, there is no significant increase in any of eight individual situations. Only one situation (Situation 14) showed marginally significant increase. In contrast, in expressing gratitude, the SA group significantly increased their mean scores in three (Situations 18, 19, and 20) out of eight situations and the increase is marginally significant in two situations (Situations 17 and 23). The AH group showed a significant increase in only one situation (Situation 7) out of the overall 24 situations. These results may suggest that positive effects of study abroad experiences are most likely to appear in expressing gratitude while they are less likely to appear in requests and refusals. In other words, expressing gratitude could be the easiest speech act to develop in a study abroad context while requests and refusals are rather difficult.

Discussion

Research Question 1
Are some speech acts easier for L2 learners to perform than other speech acts?

The results of the data analysis show that the speech act of requesting is the most difficult for L2 learners to perform among the three speech acts. A possible reason for the relative difficulty of requests is that there are many politeness levels with various conventional expressions (i.e., pragmatic routines) for requests. The speaker has to choose the most appropriate politeness level and routine according to the context, such as the interlocuter's status and the imposition. The production by the NE students shows that they often use 'can I' and 'can you' in the situations where the interlocutor's status is equal and the imposition is low. When the interlocutor's status or the imposition is higher, they use politer routines, such as 'could you' and 'do/would you mind'. In the situations where both the interlocutor's status and the imposition are high, they use more polite routines, such as 'I was wondering if' and 'would it be possible'. Although native speakers can use these routines almost automatically, it is difficult for L2 learners to do that due to their limited pragmalinguistic resources and insufficient control capacity. They may not be familiar with those routines, or even if they know them, they have difficulty automatically using syntactically complex expressions, such as 'I was wondering if' and 'do/would you mind'. As the author described in Osuka (2017)[1], Japanese learners tend to depend on a limited number of specific expressions, such as *please* + imperative', 'can I', and 'could you', regardless of the context when they make a request. As a result, their politeness is not sufficient in some situations, such as higher-status and high-imposition situations.

The speech act of refusing seems to be also difficult for L2 learners to perform appropriately. This difficulty is partly due to the complex nature of refusals. As indicated in the previous section, the speech act of refusal responds to various speech acts such as offers, invitations, requests, and suggestions. Therefore, the speaker has to change the way of refusing according to the preceding speech act as well as the interlocutor's status and the imposition. He or she would express gratitude to an offer, an invitation or a suggestion before or after refusing (e.g., *No, thank you.*). He or she would give an apology when refusing a request (e.g., *Sorry, I'll be busy on that day*.). The data from the current study suggest that Japanese learners often give an apology in the situation where native speakers usually express gratitude. (e.g., *Sorry, I'm not hungry.*)

Another difficulty of refusing is the inconsistent patterns of refusals. When making a refusal, speakers may use direct refusals, such as 'no' and 'I can't', or indirect refusals, such as 'I'll be busy on that day' and 'I'm fine' to make a refusal. They often use both direct and indirect refusals in one utterance. For example, there are two direct refusals and two indirect refusals in the following utterance.

"<u>No</u>. <u>I'm sorry</u> <u>I can't</u>. <u>I have another appointment</u>."
　direct　　indirect　　direct　　　　　indirect

Thus, unlike requests or expressing gratitude, there is often more than one head act[2] in refusals. It would be difficult for learners to work appropriately with this kind of complicated structure in varying situations.

On the other hand, expressing gratitude is easier for learners to perform probably because of the constant use of an IFID (illocutionary force indicating device), such as 'thank you', 'thanks', and 'appreciate'. One of these IFIDs is almost always used when expressing gratitude. The consistent patterns and the limited choices of IFIDs could make expressing gratitude easier for learners to perform. In fact, all the appropriateness scores are over 3 in all the expressing-gratitude situations for both the SA and AH groups.

Research Question 2

Are some speech acts easier for L2 learners to develop in a study abroad context than other speech acts?

Although the SA group demonstrated significant development in all the three speech acts, some differences were found in their development in each speech act. The results suggest that expressing gratitude is also easier to develop than the other two speech acts.

These differences may be attributed to the different amounts of exposure to each speech act during the sojourn in the target country. Expressing gratitude is a speech act that people are likey to use every day, for small or large favours. As long as we live in a community, we may not be able to have even one day without expressing gratitude. It is easy to imagine that SA students had abundant exposure and many opportunities to express it during their sojourn. That is probably one of the main reasons why they could demonstrate considerable development in their performance of this speech act. On the other hand, SA students seem to have fewer opportunities to use requests or refusals. Although they may have many opportunities to hear or make a request for a small thing, they probably have few chances to hear or make a request for a big one, as McGroarty and Taguchi (2005) stated. This could be the case with refusals.

It seems that the differences of learners' development among the three speech acts are also related to their acquisition of pragmatic routines. As Osuka (2017) describes, many Japanese learners acquired the routines 'thank you so much' and 'I (really) appreciate' during the sojourn in the target country. Although they did not use 'thank you so much' frequently before studying abroad, after their return, there was a remarkable increase in their use of this routine. They used it in many situations regardless of the context, and 'thank you so much' is basically applicable to any kind of situation. Similar to native speakers, some students used 'I (really) appreciate' in situations where the interlocutor's status and/or the imposition was high. Using these routines may make their utterances sound more native-like and significantly increase the appropriateness scores when expressing gratitude.

In requests, as indicated above, SA students showed a tendency to depend on specific expressions. Although they heavily used '*please* + imperative' for requesting before studying abroad, they almost completely stopped using it after studying abroad. Instead, they mostly used 'can I' and 'could you' after studying abroad. Many of them used 'can I' in Situation 3 [notes] and 'could you' in Situation 6 [louder]. As described in Osuka (2017), these are very similar to the tendencies of native speakers. This can explain why the SA group's increase of the appropriateness mean score was significant in Situation 6 and marginally significant in Situation 3. However, the problem is that, even after studying abroad, SA students often used 'can I' and 'could you' in the situations where native speakers usually use politer expressions such as 'I was wondering if' and 'do/would you mind' (e.g., *Could you write a recommendation for me?*). This is probably one of the reasons why their appropriateness scores are still rather low in higher-status and high-imposition situations after studying abroad.

In refusals, the SA group did not show any significant increase in any situation. This also could be related to their non-use of pragmatic routines. As stated in Osuka (2017), Japanese learners did not acquire any pragmatic routines in refusals in a study abroad context. They sometimes used 'no thank you', but 'no thank you' is applicable to only a limited range of situations. Many routines in refusals are situation-specific and learners seem to have limited opportunities to be exposed to those routines. The lack of useful pragmatic routines in refusals probably makes it difficult for learners to develop this particular speech act.

Conclusion

Although this study was carefully conducted, there are some limitations in this study. First, the data was elicited through an instrument with a one-turn format. Therefore, their utterances could be different from what learners would say in natural situations where speakers attain a communicative goal over multiple turns. Another limitation is the small size of each group. As is often the case with longitudinal studies, it was difficult for the researcher to collect a large number of participants. Therefore, more empirical research is necessary in order to generalize the findings.

In spite of these limitations, some important implications may be derived from this study on the effects of speech acts on learners' pragmatic development in a study abroad context. Although the results of the appropriateness assessment indicate that study abroad experiences have positive effects on learners' pragmatic development in all the three speech acts, a comparison among these speech acts indicates that requests and refusals are more difficult for learners to perform and develop than expressing gratitude. This could be related to the different nature of each speech act and learners' acquisition of pragmatic routines in each speech act. The speech act which has a rather simple structure and whose routines are applicable to various contexts, such as expressing gratitude, is easier to perform and develop. The speech acts which have a rather complex structure and/or whose routines are applicable to a limited range of contexts, such as requests and refusals, are more difficult. The varying amounts of exposure to each speech act during the sojourn in the target country could also be related to the different development of the three speech acts. Study abroad students are more likely to be exposed to expressing gratitude in everyday life during the sojourn than to requests and refusals. Probably this abundant exposure makes expressing gratitude easier for learners to develop than the other two speech acts.

One semester could be too short a period to develop learners' pragmatic ability to appropriately perform difficult speech acts such as requests and refusals. However, many students choose a one-semester study abroad program for a variety of reasons, including financial reasons. Pragmatic instruction prior to or while studying abroad might be able to be a solution to enhance the effects of studying abroad. Further research is needed to explore the possibility.

References

Bardovi-Harlig, K., & Bastos, M.-T. (2011). Proficiency, length of stay, and intensity of interaction and the acquisition of conventional expressions in L2 pragmatics. *Intercultural Pragmatics*, 8, 347-384.

Bardovi-Harlig, K., & Dörnyei, Z. (1998). Do language learners recognize pragmatic variations? Pragmatic versus grammatical awareness in instructed L2 learning. *TESOL Quarterly*, 32 (2), 233-262.

Barron, A. (2003). *Acquisition in interlanguage pragmatics: Learning how to do things with words in a study abroad context*. Amsterdam: Benjamins.

Bataller, R. (2010). Making a request for a service in Spanish: Pragmatic development in the study abroad setting. *Foreign Language Annals*, 43 (1), 160-175.

Beebe, L. M., Takahashi, T., & Uliss-Weltz, R. (1990). Pragmatic transfer in ESL refusals. In R. C. Scarcella, E. S. Andersen & S. D. Krashen (Eds.), *Developing communicative competence in a second language* (pp. 55-73). New York, NY: Newbury House.

Blum-Kulka, S., House, J., & Kasper, G. (1989). *Cross-cultural pragmatics: Requests and apologies.* Norwood, NJ: Ablex.

Blum-Kulka, S., & Olshtain, E. (1986). Too many words: Length of utterance and pragmatic failure. *Studies in Second Language Acquisition,* 8 (2), 165-179.

Brown, P., & Levinson, S. C. (1987). *Politeness: Some universals in language usage.* Cambridge: Cambridge University Press.

Clankie, S. M. (1993). The use of expressions of gratitude in English by Japanese and American university students. *The Review of Inquiry and Research,* Kansai Gaidai University, 58, 37-71.

Cohen, A. & Shvely, R. L. (2007). Acquisition of requests and apologies in Spanish and French: Impact of study abroad and strategy-building intervention. *The Modern Language Journal,* 91 (2), 189-212.

Eisenstein, M., & Bodman, J. W. (1993). Expressing gratitude in American English. In G. Kasper & S. Blum-Kulka (Eds.), *Interlanguage pragmatics* (pp. 64-81). New York, NY: Oxford University Press.

Félix-Brasdefer, J. C. (2004). Interlanguage refusals: Linguistic politeness and length of residence in the target community. *Language Learning,* 54 (4), 587-653.

Félix-Brasdefer, J. C. (2010). Data collection methods in speech act performance: DCTs, role plays, and verbal reports. In E. Usó Juán & A. Martínez-Flor (Eds.), *Speech act performance: Theoretical, empirical, and methodological issues* (pp. 41-56). Amsterdam: John Benjamins Publishing.

Hoffman-Hicks, S. D. (2000). *The longitudinal development of French foreign language pragmatic competence: Evidence from study abroad participants.* Unpublished doctoral dissertation, Indiana University, Bllomington.

Kasper, G., & Schmidt, R. (1996). Developmental issues in interlanguage pragmatics. *Studies in Second Language Acquisition,* 18 (2), 149-169.

Kasper, G., & Rose, K. R. (2002). *Pragmatic development in a second language.* Malden, MA: Blackwell.

Leech, G. N. (2014). *The pragmatics of politeness.* New York, NY: Oxford University Press.

Matsumura, S. (2001). Learning the rules for offering advice: A quantitative approach to second language socialization. *Language Learning*, 51 (4), 635-679.

Matsumura, S. (2003). Modeling the relationships among interlanguage pragmatic development, L2 proficiency, and exposure to L2. *Applied Linguistics*, 24 (4), 465-491.

McGroarty, M., & Taguchi, N. (2005). Evaluating communicativeness of EFL textbooks for Japanese secondary schools. In J. Frodesen & C. Holten (Eds.), *The power of context in language teaching and learning* (pp. 211-224). Boston, MA: Thomson/Heinle & Heinle.

Nakai, M. (2004). Pragmatic transfers in interlanguage expressions of gratitude in the age of World Englishes. *Gogaku Kyouiku Kenkyuu Ronsou*, Daito Bunka University, 21, 167-184.

Osuka, N. (2017). Development of pragmatic routines by Japanese learners in a study abroad context. In I. Kecskes and S. Assimakopoulos (Eds.) *Current issues in intercultural pragmatics* (pp. 275-296). Amsterdam/Philadelphia: John Benjamins Publishing Company.

Rose, K. R., & Ono, R. (1995). Eliciting speech act data in Japanese: The effect of questionnaire type. *Language Learning*, 45 (2), 191-223.

Sasaki, M. (1998). Investigating EFL students' production of speech acts: A comparison of production questionnaires and role plays. *Journal of Pragmatics*, 30 (4), 457-484.

Schauer, G. A. (2004). May you speak louder maybe? Interlanguage pragmatic development in requests. In S. H. Foster-Cohen, M. Sharwood Smith, A. Sorace & M. Ota (Eds.), *EUROSLA Yearbook*, vol. 4 (pp. 253-273). Amsterdam: John Benjamins.

Schauer, G. A. (2009). *Interlanguage pragmatic development: The study abroad context*. London: Continuum.

Shively, R. L. (2011). L2 Pragmatic development in study abroad: A longitudinal study of Spanish service encounters. *Journal of Pragmatics*, 43, 1818-1835.

Taguchi, N. (2011a). Do proficiency and study-abroad experience affect speech act production? Analysis of appropriateness, accuracy, and fluency. *International Review of Applied Linguistics*, 49, 265-293.

Taguchi, N. (2011b). Rater variation in the assessment of speech acts. *Pragmatics*, 21, 453-471.

Notes

[1] This study focuses on the development of pragmatic routines by Japanese learners in a study abroad context. It uses the same instrument (i.e., MET), but the number of the participants (16 SA students) is smaller than that of the current study (22 SA students).

[2] The head act is the "part of the sequence which might serve to realize the act independently of other elements" (Blum-Kulka & Olshtain, 1984). For example, in the request sequence "Hey, I missed class yesterday. Can I borrow your notes?", the part "Can I borrow your notes" is the head act.

Investigating the Effects of Short-Term Study Abroad on the Listenership of Japanese EFL University Students

Pino Cutrone and Keisuke Imamura

Abstract

The purpose of this study is to measure the effect of study abroad on one aspect of learners' pragmatic competence, listenership. A total of 20 Japanese university students participated in this study. Each student was given pragmatic tests at three points in time: within four to seven days of going abroad, within seven days of returning to Japan, and four to five weeks later. Each of these tests involved participating in an intercultural conversation with a native speaker of English, and being interviewed. To determine the efficacy of preparatory instruction, half of the students set to study abroad were given explicit instruction on listenership. The results of this study point to the benefits of study abroad, particularly on the learners who received instruction prior to studying abroad. The students who received pre-SA instruction on listenership were able to sustain the instructional goal of sending minimal backchannels less frequently (especially while one's interlocutor was speaking) and extended backchannels more frequently, with greater variability (but at context-appropriate moments), while asking questions and taking the primary speakership in the conversation more often, and initiating conversational repair strategies when they did not understand and/or disagree rather than feign understanding and agreement.

Keywords: study abroad (SA), pragmatics, listenership, Japanese EFL context, willingness to communicate (WTC)

Introduction

This paper attempts to shed light on two important aspects of foreign language education: study abroad and pragmatic competence. Concerning the former, it is not always clear what students gain from study abroad experiences in terms of foreign language outcomes. Broadly speaking, there has been a general assumption that studying abroad is the best way to learn a foreign language. However, as Tanaka and Ellis (2003) found in their survey of the research literature in this area, this assumption may require a great deal of qualification. For instance, much of the research to date suggests that study abroad may not necessarily yield better results than classroom instruction where grammar, listening and reading are concerned, particularly with higher-level students (Freed, 1998).

Specifically, as it relates to the study of pragmatic competence in this study, an important aspect of effective oral communication is being able to give adequate feedback to one's interlocutor. This conversational skill-set is known as *Listenership* and is one of the areas in which Japanese EFL speakers (JEFLs hereafter) have been shown to struggle with (Cutrone, 2005, 2014). A number of studies into this phenomenon have shown that the listenership of Japanese EFL speakers differs to that of proficient English speakers from other cultures in many respects (Cutrone 2005, 2014; Maynard, 1997; White, 1989), and such differences can lead to miscommunication, negative perceptions and stereotyping across cultures (Cutrone, 2005, 2014; LoCastro, 1987). Despite the aforementioned importance of listenership in intercultural communication, this aspect of pragmatic competence remains largely neglected in EFL classes in Japan (Capper, 2000; Cutrone, 2016a). There has, however, been some speculation that study abroad might have an especially positive influence on learner's pragmatic competence (Tanaka & Ellis, 2003). Thus, in an effort to inform foreign language pedagogy, the purpose of this study is to examine the effects of study abroad on the listenership of Japanese EFL learners.

Identifying Key Features of Listenership

First, in defining the key term used in this study, McCarthy (2003) develops the notion of active *Listenership* as a conversational skill. Listenership refers to the use of appropriate response tokens (which are commonly referred to as *backchannels*), and other expressions to acknowledge, react and engage with the contribution of another speaker. Backchannels (BCs) may range from brief vocalizations/backchannels (such as *uhuh* and *mm*) to longer responses with more affective content such as evaluations (i.e., *that's right* and *how cool*) to return questions and/or conversational repair strategies (such as *I beg your pardon* and *what do you mean by that*). Following the primary writer's earlier work (Cutrone, 2005, 2010, 2014), aspects of listenership are divided into the categories presented below.

Observations

The first area, observations, refers to the sub-features of listenership that can be observed, quantified and compared across cultures. These sub-features include frequency, variability, discourse contexts, and the form and function of listener responses. The following will examine each sub-category more closely and suggest a direction for effective listenership behaviour in each area. Concerning the latter, directions for effective listenership were based on two goals: trying to approximate the listenership behaviour of fully proficient speakers of English, and taking into account the issues that JEFLs have been known to have where listenership is concerned.

Frequency. Various studies have observed JEFLs sending backchannel up to four times more frequently than proficient speakers of English (Cutrone, 2005, 2014; Maynard, 1997; White, 1989). Thus, one target for JEFLs would be to backchannel less frequently.

Variability. There is also evidence of JEFLs relying on non-verbal and/or brief non-word vocalisations (i.e., minimal backchannels) in their intercultural conversations in English (Cutrone 2005, 2014). Hence, in approximating proficient speakers of English, another target for JEFLs would be to try to employ a more varied and diverse repertoire of listener responses in their conversations in English (i.e., extended backchannels). In specific terms, *minimal responses* are identified in this study as any non-lexical and/or non-verbal listener response (i.e., including backchannels such as head nods and *mhm, uhuh, nn,* etc) occurring in isolation. *Extended responses,* in contrast, are identified in this study as the lengthier verbal listener feedback consisting of multiple and varied words (i.e., expressions) irrespective of nonverbal backchannel accompaniment.

Discourse contexts. This area refers to the places in the primary speaker's speech that the listener sends backchannels. For instance, JEFLs and proficient speakers of English alike tend to send backchannels at grammatical completion points and/or pauses in the primary speaker's speech (Cutrone, 2005, 2014; Maynard, 1997; White, 1989). However, where simultaneous speech (i.e., backchannels that overlap with the primary speaker's speech) is concerned, JEFLs sent backchannels far more frequently. As these frequent JEFL simultaneous speech backchannels are sometimes interpreted as interruptions (Cutrone, 2005, 2014; Maynard 1997), another suggested target for JEFLs is to backchannel less frequently when their interlocutor is speaking.

Form and function. Ideally, the form that a listener sends should correspond to the function that they intend to convey and, most importantly, their form/function should be received and understood by their interlocutor as such. One potential problem concerning JEFLs where function is concerned is the tendency to use unconventional backchannel forms (i.e., continuer and agreement type backchannels) in situations of non-understanding and/or disagreement. Cutrone (2005, 2014) found that the primary JEFL strategy for dealing with non-understanding and/or disagreement in his studies was to feign understanding, and this sometimes led to communication breakdown. Therefore, one target for JEFLs is to feign understanding and/or agreement less in these situations and instead use conversational repair strategies and management techniques to try to overcome these tricky situations.

Research Questions

Research into L2 listenership behaviour, and particularly how it is affected by such factors as study abroad, is in its infancy and, thus, much remains unknown. Accordingly, in an attempt to shed light on this aspect of L2 Listenership, Research Question (RQ) 1 is formulated as follows:

RQ 1: What are the effects of short-term study abroad (SA) on the listenership of Japanese EFL university students (JEFLs)?

Further, in an effort to look for ways to increase what students can gain in their time abroad where listenership is concerned, RQ 2 examines the effect of pre-SA instruction, as follows:

RQ 2: What are the effects of pre-SA instruction on the listenership of JEFLs upon returning from SA?

In short, by providing a thorough account of how SA (as well as pre-SA instruction) affects L2 listenership over time, this study has two main aims: to help researchers gain a better understanding of how short-term SA affects pragmatic competence, and to help SA administrators and/or instructors better prepare their students for success when they SA.

Methodology

This section describes the methodology of this study. This includes information pertaining to the participants of this study, methods for collecting data, as well as the procedures and time schedule for this study.

Participants

The study included 24 participants that were involved in three capacities. First, in the student participant capacity (i.e., JEFLs), this study involved 20 freshmen at a national university in southern Japan (16 females and 4 males), who were enrolled in a faculty that focuses on English studies and cultural diversity. At the beginning of the study, JEFLs were between 18 and 20 years old and were at an intermediate level of English proficiency or higher (as reflected by their TOEFL PBT scores). Second, in the conversational partner capacity, this study included two native speakers of English (1 female and 1 male) to serve as interlocutors in the intercultural dyadic conversations with the JEFLs. All participants were given explicit instructions (i.e., verbal and written, in both English and Japanese) regarding this study and their role in it.

Data Collection Methods

The data in this study was collected through observations and interviews. First, observations were carried out by video recording intercultural dyadic conversations (conducted in English) between a JEFL and a native English speaker (NES). These conversations took place in the primary researcher's office, and only the conversational participants were present when the recording occurred. Participants were recorded for fifteen minutes (using a Sony digital video camera, Model FDR AX100), of which the middle five was used as conversational data. Conversational prompts were given to help start the conversation, but participants were told they could speak about anything they like. The video-recorded conversations were transcribed and subsequently analyzed for patterns in the above-mentioned areas (i.e., frequency, variability, discourse contexts, form and functions of listener responses). Additionally, post-conversation reflective interviews were used to dig deeper into the JEFLs' thought process concerning listenership behaviour. Interviews consisted of each JEFL watching a recording of their conversation and answering the primary researcher's questions.

Procedures and Time Schedule of This Study

As shown in Table 1, the 20 student participants were each given pragmatic tests at three points in time: within five days of going abroad (pretest), within five days of returning to Japan (post-test 1), and approximately one month later (i.e., post-test 2, the delayed post-test). Each test was identical and involved participating in an intercultural conversation with a NES and being interviewed by the researcher. Furthermore, to determine the efficacy of preparatory instruction, half of the students set to study abroad (N = 10) were given explicit instruction on listenership before they departed. This consisted of two (2-hour) instructional sessions focusing on the following strategies: consciousness raising activities used to draw students' attention to various features of conversation (i.e., frequency, variability, discourse contexts and form and function of listener responses), discussions

Table 1
Schedule of the Study

Aspect of study	Time administered
Pre-SA Evaluations (observation/questionnaire/interview)	4-7 days before study abroad
Group A receives Instruction on Listenership	2-3 days before study abroad
Groups A and B Study Abroad	Duration: 3.5 weeks of study abroad
Post-SA Evaluations (observation/questionnaire/interview)	1-7 days after returning from study abroad
Delayed Post-SA Evaluations (observation/questionnaire/interview)	4-5 weeks after returning from study abroad

on the implications of cross-cultural communication styles, exposure to models demonstrating effective listenership in a host of situations in English, and, ultimately, practice opportunities with subsequent corrective feedback.

The study abroad experiences of Groups A and B were similar across the board. As shown in Table 2, each group enrolled in separate study abroad programs for three and a half weeks in major universities in central Canada. Both programs provided 24 hours of ESL classroom instruction per week which focused on the development of the four major skills of language competence (i.e. Reading, Writing, Listening and Speaking). In addition, both programs provided a range of extracurricular (EC) activities, which included educational field trips to historical and cultural landmarks, sightseeing trips, group shopping excursions, participating and/or attending sporting events and parties with local and international students, etc. Lastly, students in both programs lived with Canadian host families, which in many cases included other international (i.e., non-Japanese) students.

Table 2
The Two Groups Used in This Study

Group	Number in each group	Location	Length	Hours of study / week	Content of study	Make-up of class members	Accomodation settings
A	10	Central Canada	3.5 weeks	24	4 skills (+ ECs)	mixed nationalities	Homestay (with other students; partially mixed nationalities)
B	10	Central Canada	3.5 weeks	24	4 skills (+ ECs)	mixed nationalities	Homestay (with other students; partially mixed nationalities)

Results

This section will report the results of the observational phase of this study. The subcategories that will be presented include frequency, variability, discourse contexts, simultaneous speech and function of backchannels.

Observations

Frequency. Tables 3 and 4 respectively present Group A and B's total backchannel (BC) output, number of their interlocutor's words, and the number of backchannels per interlocutor word during the Pre-test, Post-test 1 and Post-test 2. Concerning the latter category, which takes into account the backchannel opportunities afforded to each conversational participant, it is useful to point out that the fewer the interlocutor words between backchannels, the more frequent the rate of backchannelling. Group A provided a backchannel every 12.24 of their interlocutor's words during the Pre-test, 13.02 during Post-test 1, and 9.44 during Post-test 2, while Group B provided a backchannel every 10.74 of their interlocutor's words during the Pre-test,

Table 3
Differences in Frequency of Backchannels Over Time for Group A

N = 10	Total backchannels			Interlocutor's words			Average number of interlocutor's words between backchannels		
	Pre	Post 1	Post 2	Pre	Post 1	Post 2	Pre	Post 1	Post 2
Total	134	92	142	1641	1198	1341	—	—	—
Mean ($\bar{x}$)	13.4	9.2	14.2	164.1	119.8	134.1	12.24	13.02	9.44
SD	10.7	5.7	9.9	78.75	52.12	68.5	11.82	9.48	5.1

($\bar{x}$ difference of Pre-test → Post-test 1, and Pre-test → Post-test 2 significant at $p<.05$ level = *; significant at $p<.01$ level =**)

Table 4
Differences in Frequency of Backchannels Over Time for Group B

N = 10	Backchannels			Interlocutor's words			Average number of interlocutor's words between backchannels		
	Pre	Post 1	Post 2	Pre	Post 1	Post 2	Pre	Post 1	Post 2
Total	144	143	144	1547	1482	1280	—	—	—
Mean (x̄)	14.4	14.3	14.4	154.7	148.2	128	10.74	10.36	8.89
SD	7.88	8.54	5.89	80.02	78.69	19.61	10.47	6.68	9.91

(x̄ difference of Pre-test → Post-test 1, and Pre-test → Post-test 2 significant at $p<.05$ level = *; significant at $p<.01$ level =**)

10.36 during Post-test 1, and 8.89 during Post-test 2.

Illustrating the path of the two groups collectively, Figure 1 shows that both groups increased their backchannel frequency from the Pre-test to Post-test 2 (Group A sent on average 2.8 fewer backchannels per interlocutor word, while Group B sent 1.85 fewer). These increases were largely negligible (and not found to be statistically significant). That is, based on the previous description of the backchannel behaviour of proficient speakers of English (Cutrone, 2010), the backchannel frequency rates of both groups were not thought to be excessive at any of the three times of measurement.

The results concerning frequency were somewhat surprising in that most of the other studies involving JEFLs had them sending backchannels far more frequently. Further, members of Group A (the group that received pre-SA instruction) were instructed to backchannel less frequently. From the Pre-test to Post-test 1, Group A did, in fact, backchannel slightly less frequently (.78 more backchannels per interlocutor word), while Group B (the group that did not receive pre-SA instruction) backchannelled slightly more frequently (.41 fewer backchannels per interlocutor word); however,

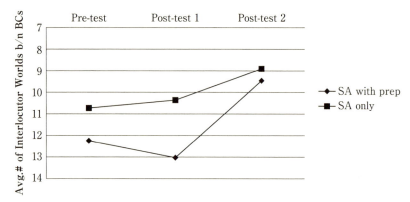

Figure 1 Comparing backchannel frequencies of the two groups over time.

ultimately, at the time of the delayed post-test (i.e., Post-test 2), the frequency rates for both groups had increased beyond their starting levels (in the Pre-test).

Variability. The results that will be presented concerning the Variability category have been limited to reporting Groups A and B's use of minimal versus extended backchannels (see section above for definition/distinction). The raw total of each sub type and the mean percentage constituted by each sub type of the total backchannels (BCs) and standard deviations (SDs) over time will be reported. Table 5 reports that the raw totals of minimal backchannels decreased from the Pre-test (107) to the Post-test 1 (57) and then increased again back to near their original level in Post-test 2 (101). Paired-samples t-tests showed that the decrease (of 50) in minimal responses from the Pre-test to Post-test 1 was statistically significant (at the .05 level). Further, Table 5 also shows that the mean percentage of Group A's backchannels that were minimal responses was 80% in the Pre-test, 62% in

Table 5
Group A's Use of Minimal Versus Extended Backchannels Over Time

N = 10	Pre-test			Post test 1			Post test 2		
Type of Back- channel	Total	x̄ % of Total BCs	SD	Total	x̄ % of Total BCs	SD	Total	x̄ % of Total BCs	SD
Minimal Response	107	80	.6	57* (p<.05)	62** (p<.01)	.7	101	71** (p<.002)	2.07
Extended Response	2	2	42	18** (p<.005)	20* (p<.025)	.55	19** (p<.000)	13	74

(x̄ difference of Pre-test → Post-test 1, and Pre-test → Post-test 2 significant at p<.05 level = *; significant at p<.01 level =**)

Post-test 1 and 71% in Post-test 2. Paired-samples t-tests confirmed that the difference between the mean percentages of total backchannels in the Pre-test and Post-test 1, and the difference between the means of the Pre-test to Post-tests 1 and 2, were statistically significant (at the .01 level). In comparison, the raw number of Group A's backchannels that were extended responses was 2 in the Pre-test, 18 in Post-test 1 and 19 in Post-test 2. The differences between the means from the Pre-test to Post-tests 1 and 2 were found to be strongly significant (at the .01 level). Moreover, the mean percentage of Group A's backchannels that were extended responses was 2% in the Pre-test, 20% in Post-test 1 and 13% in Post-test 2. The difference between the means from the Pre-test to Post-test 1 was also found to be statistically significant (at the .05 level).

Regarding Group B's use of minimal versus extended responses, Table 6 shows that, similar to the path of Group A, the raw totals of minimal backchannels decreased from the Pre-test (131) to the Post-test 1 (94) and then increased again back to near their original level in Post-test (110). Further,

Table 6
Group B's Use of Minimal Versus Extended Backchannels Over Time

N = 10	Pre-test			Post test 1			Post test 2		
Type of Backchannel	Total	x̄ % of Total BCs	SD	Total	x̄ % of Total BCs	SD	Total	x̄ % of Total BCs	SD
Minimal Response	131	91	8.36	94	66	.36	110	76	.9
Extended Response	3	2	48	2	8.4	.23	9* (*p*<.04)	6.3	57

(x̄ difference of Pre-test → Post-test 1, and Pre-test → Post-test 2 significant at *p*<.05 level = *; significant at *p*<.01 level =**)

the mean percentage of Group B's backchannels that were minimal responses was 91% in the Pre-test, 66% in Post-test 1 and 76% in Post-test 2. Comparatively, the raw number of Group B's backchannels that were extended responses was 3 in the Pre-test, 12 in Post-test 1 and 9 in Post-test 2. The difference between the means from the Pre-test to Post-test 2 was found to be statistically significant (at the .05 level). Moreover, the mean percentage of Group B's backchannels that were extended responses was 2% in the Pre-test, 8.4% in Post-test 1 and 6.3% in Post-test 2.

The data illustrated in Figures 2 and 3 compare the two groups' use of minimal and extended responses respectively over time. As Figure 2 illustrates, the general paths of Groups A and B mirrored one another where the percentages of BCs as minimal responses were concerned. That is, both groups' BCs were comprised mostly of minimal responses (80% and 91% respectively) at the Pre-test, then both groups noticeably decreased their reliance on minimal responses (thus, showing improvement) at the Post-test 1 (by 18% and 25% respectively), and, ultimately at the Post-test 2, both

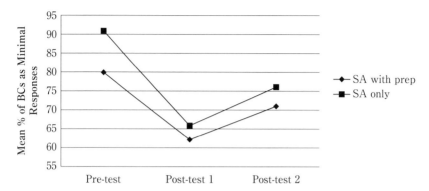

Figure 2 Comparing the proportions of minimal backchannels over time.

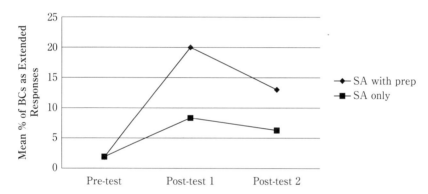

Figure 3 Comparing the proportions of extended backchannels over time.

groups showed increases from their Post-test 1 levels 1 (by 9% and 10% respectively) but still lower than their original Pre-test levels (by 9% and 15% respectively).

Figure 3 highlights some noticeable differences in terms of the two groups' use of extended backchannels over time. While both groups were able to make gains in this area, it is clear to see that Group A showed far greater improvement overall. Both groups rarely used extended backchannels at all at the time of the Pre-test; however, at Post-test 1, the percentage of Group A's BCs that were extended BCs rose significantly by 18%, while that of Group B rose by 6.4%. Finally, at the Post-test 2, both groups showed decreases from their Post-test 1 levels (by 7% and 2.1% respectively) but still much higher than their original Pre-test levels (by 11% and 4.3% respectively).

Discourse contexts. Focusing on the primary discourse contexts of backchannels, Tables 7 and 8 respectively report two main statistics regarding the clausal boundaries (CBs) of Groups A and B's backchannels at the three tests: (1) the mean percentage of opportunities (Opps) that CBs attracted backchannels (with SDs), and (2) the mean percentage of backchannels constituted by CBs (with SDs). As reported in Table 7, Group A sent BCs in 38% of the opportunities presented to them in the Pre-test, 32.7% in Post-test 1, and 38% in Post-test 2. Further, the mean percentage of Group A's total BCs that were sent at or near CBs were 64.41% in the Pre-test, 67.87% at Post-test 1, and 73.03% at Post-test 2.

As reported in Table 8, Group B sent BCs in 27.76% of the opportunities

Table 7
Discourse Contexts of Group A's Backchannels Over Time

N = 10	Pre-test		Post test 1		Post test 2	
Discourse Contexts	x̄ % of Opps (SD)	x̄ % of BCs (SD)	x̄ % of Opps (SD)	x̄ % of BCs (SD)	x̄ % of Opps (SD)	x̄ % of BCs (SD)
At or near final CB	38 (22.06)	64.41 (28.31)	32.7 (10.16)	67.87 (13)	38 (9.59)	73.03 (12.73)

(x̄ difference of Pre-test → Post-test 1, and Pre-test → Post-test 2 significant at $p<.05$ level = *; significant at $p<.01$ level =**)

Table 8
Discourse Contexts of Group B's Backchannels Over Time

N = 10	Pre-test		Post test 1		Post test 2	
Discourse Context	x̄ % of Opps (SD)	x̄ % of BCs (SD)	x̄ % of Opps (SD)	x̄ % of BCs (SD)	x̄ % of Opps (SD)	x̄ % of BCs (SD)
At or near final CB	27.76 (3.7)	66.51 (26.16)	28.13 (6.98)	64.14 (18.08)	33.9* ($p<.039$) (6.13)	65.01 (17.55)

(x̄ difference of Pre-test → Post-test 1, and Pre-test → Post-test 2 significant at $p<.05$ level = *; significant at $p<.01$ level =**)

presented to them in the Pre-test, 28.13% in Post-test 1, and 33.9% in Post-Test 2. The 6.14% increase from the Pre-test to Post-test 2 was found to be statistically significant at the .05 level. Further, the mean percentage of Group B's total BCs that were sent at or near CBs were 66.51% in the Pre-test, 64.14% at Post-test 1, and 65.01% at Post-test 2.

Figure 4 illustrates the differences in how frequently Groups A and B sent backchannels at final clause boundaries. Comparisons between the two groups show that Group A started out much higher and performed better overall, while Group B appeared to make greater strides in this area over time. The percentage of BCs Group A sent at CBs decreased from the Pre-test to Post-test 1 (by 5.3%) and then reverted back to their Pre-test level in Post-test 2 (i.e., 38%). Members of Group B, on the other hand, increased the percentage of BCs they sent at CBs from the Pre-test to Post-test 1 by .37%, and then by 5.77% from the Post-test 1 to the Post-test 2.

Figure 5 shows the differences in the proportions of Group A and B's total BCs that were comprised of backchannels sent at final clause boundaries. While both groups had similar outputs in the Pre-test, it is clear to see

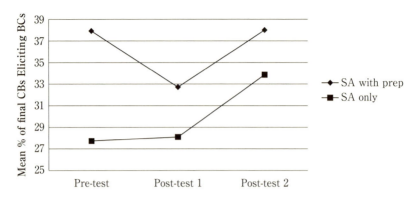

Figure 4 Comparing the proportions of final clause boundaries attracting BCs.

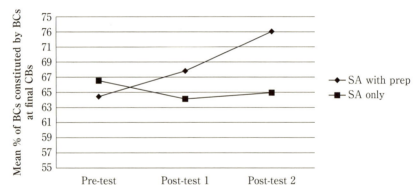

Figure 5 Comparing the proportions of BCs constituted by BCs at final CBs.

that Group A made greater strides in this area over time. The proportions for Group A increased from the Pre-test to Post-tests 1 and 2 by 3.46% and 8.62% respectively, whereas it decreased for Group B from the Pre-test to Post-tests 1 and 2 by 2.37% and 1.5% respectively.

Simultaneous speech backchannels (SSBs). Tables 9 and 10 respectively report on Group A and B's use of simultaneous speech backchannels (SSBs), which include the mean scores and standard deviations of each group, and the mean percentage of total backchannels constituted by SSBs (with SDs) in the three tests. As shown in Table 9, the average number of SSBs decreased significantly from the Pre-test to Post-test 1 (at the .05 level) for Group A; however, this decrease was only partially sustained at the Post-test 2, as the average number of SSBs increased from Post-test 1 to the Post-test 2 by .7. In addition, paired-samples t-tests comparing the decreases in the mean percentage of backchannels constituted by SSBs from the

Table 9
SSBs of Group A Over Time

N = 10	Pre-test			Post-test 1			Post-test 2		
—	Total	x̄ (SD)	x̄ % of BCs (SD)	Total	x̄ (SD)	x̄ % of BCs (SD)	Total	x̄ (SD)	x̄ % of BCs (SD)
Total SSBs	22	2.2 (1.87)	18.8 (17.33)	6	.6* ($p<.041$)	9.7 (11.43) .52	13	1.3 (1.3)	9.1* ($p<.049$) (7.46)

(x̄ difference of Pre-test → Post-test 1, and Pre-test → Post-test 2 significant at $p<.05$ level = *; significant at $p<.01$ level = **)

Table 10
SSBs of Group B Over Time

N = 10	Pre-test			Post-test 1			Post-test 2		
T	Total	x̄ (SD)	x̄ % of BCs (SD)	Total	x̄ (SD)	x̄ % of BCs (SD)	Total	x̄ (SD)	x̄ % of BCs (SD)
Total SSBs	22	2.2 (1.69)	21.8 (28.73)	28	2.8 (2.57)	17.1 (2.57)	25	2.5 (11.89)	17.6 (9.79)

(x̄ difference of Pre-test → Post-test 1, and Pre-test → Post-test 2 significant at $p<.05$ level = *; significant at $p<.01$ level = **)

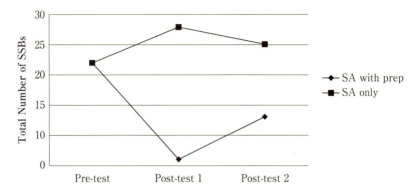

Figure 6 Comparing SSBs between the two groups over time.

Pre-test to Post-test 2 were found to be statistically significant (at the .05 level) for Group A. As shown in Table 10, there were no significant changes in the average numbers of SSBs and the mean percentage of total backchannels constituted by SSBs for Group B over time.

Figure 6 compares the total number of SSBs used by Groups A and B over time. Clearly, the path each group followed was quite different, as Group A improved in this area while Group B did not. Members of Group A (the group that received pre-SA instruction) were instructed to send SSBs less frequently, which is what they ended up doing over time. The number of SSBs sent by Group A decreased from the Pre-test to Post-test 2 (by 9), whereas the number of SSBs sent by Group B increased from the Pre-test to Post-test 2 (by 3).

Function. Tables 11 and 12 respectively report on what members of Groups A and B did when they did not understand. Table 11 shows that the mean percentage of non-understanding situations (NONUs) in which unconventional backchannels were employed by Group A was 100% in the Pre-

Table 11
Reactions at Points of Non-Understanding for Group A Over Time

N = 10	NONUs	Unconventional BCs		Conversational Repair Strategies			
				Minimal BCs		Lengthier expressions	
		Total	x̄ % of NONUs (SD)	Total	x̄ % of NONUs (SD)	Total	x̄ % of NONUs (SD)
Pre	14	14	100 (21.08)	0	0 (0)	0	0 (0)
Post 1	9	4	44* ($p<.04$) (47.43)	2	22 (21.08)	3	33* ($p<.031$) (33.54)
Post 2	13	2	15* ($p<.019$) (42.16)	5	39* ($p<.024$) (34.96)	6	46** ($p<.004$) (41.04)

(x̄ difference of Pre-test → Post-test 1, and Pre-test → Post-test 2 significant at $p<.05$ level = *; significant at $p<.01$ level =**)

test, but only 44% in Post-test 1 and 15% in Post-test 2. Paired-samples t-tests found the difference between the means from the Pre-test to Post-tests 1 and 2 to be statistically significant (at the .05 level). Further demonstrating the benefits of pre-SA instruction, Table 11 also shows that the mean percentage of non-understanding situations in which Group A employed conversational repair strategies (CRSs) rose in each test. Specifically, the mean percentage of minimal BCs used as a CRS rose by 22% and 39% from the Pre-test to Post-tests 1 and 2 respectively. The difference between the means of the Pre-test (0) and Post-test 2 (39) was found to be statistically significant at the .05 level ($p<.024$). Similarly, the mean percentage of lengthier expressions used as a CRS rose by 33% and 46% from the Pre-

Table 12

Reactions at Points of Non-Understanding for Group B Over Time

N = 10	NONUs	Unconventional BCs		Conversational Repair Strategies			
				Minimal BCs		Lengthier expressions	
		Total	x̄ % of NONUs (SD)	Total	x̄ % of NONUs (SD)	Total	x̄ % of NONUs (SD)
Pre	23	22	96 (49.93)	0	0 (0)	0	0 (0)
Post 1	14	11	79 (45.65)	2	14* ($p<.0425$) (19.1)	1	.7 (16.58)
Post 2	16	9	56 (38.34)	6	38** ($p<.006$) (37.26)	1	.6 (16.58)

(x̄ difference of Pre-test → Post-test 1, and Pre-test → Post-test 2 significant at $p<.05$ level = *; significant at $p<.01$ level =**)

test to Post-tests 1 and 2 respectively. The difference between the means of the Pre-test (0) and Post-test 1 (36) was found to be statistically significant at the .05 level ($p<.031$), and the difference between the means of the Pre-test (0) and Post-test 2 (46) was found to be strongly significant at the .01 level ($p<.004$).

Table 12 reports that the mean percentage of non-understanding situations (NONUs) in which unconventional backchannels were employed by Group B was 96% in the Pre-test, but only 79% in Post-test 1 and 56% in Post-test 2. Moreover, the mean percentage of minimal BCs used as a CRS rose by 14% and 38% from the Pre-test to Post-tests 1 and 2 respectively. The difference between the means of the Pre-test (0) and Post-test 1 (14) was found to be statistically significant at the .05 level ($p<.0425$), and the difference between the means of the Pre-test (0) and Post-test 2 (38) was found to be strongly significant at the .01 level ($p<.006$). Furthermore, the mean percentage of lengthier expressions used as a CRS rose slightly (by .7% and .6%) from the Pre-test to Post-tests 1 and 2 respectively. Finally, it is important to point out that there was one NONU in the Pre-test where a member of Group B simply remained silent (and, thus, no unconventional BC or CRS was recorded for this instance).

Figures 7-9 compare the reactions of Groups A and B in situations of NONU. While Group B was able to show some moderate improvement in various aspects of function, this was another category in which Group A clearly exhibited far greater initial and sustained improvements. As Figure 7 demonstrates, both groups used unconventional BCs in most of the NON-Us they experienced in the Pre-test; however, Group A was able to reduce this greatly by 66% and 85% in Post-tests 1 and 2 respectively, while Group B decreased the percentage of unconventional BCs they sent by 17% and

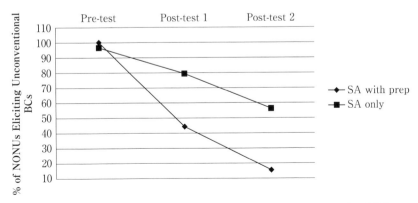

Figure 7 Comparing non-understanding situations eliciting unconventional BCs.

40% in Post-tests 1 and 2 respectively.

Figure 8 compares the frequency in which members of Groups A and B were able to produce minimal CRSs in situations of NONUs. It is clear to see that both groups showed great improvement in this area. From the Pre-test, the percentage of Group A's minimal CRSs at NONUs increased by 22% and 39% at Post-tests 1 and 2 respectively. Similarly, from the Pre-test, the percentage of Group B's minimal CRSs at NONUs increased by 14% and 38% at Post-tests 1 and 2 respectively.

Figure 9 compares the frequency in which members of Groups A and B were able to produce lengthier expressions as CRSs in situations of NONUs. This is an area in which Group A improved greatly over time, whereas Group B did not. From the Pre-test, the percentage of Group A's lengthier CRSs at NONUs increased by 33% and 46% at Post-tests 1 and 2 respectively. In contrast, from the Pre-test, the percentage of Group B's minimal CRSs at NONUs remained fairly stable, showing only slight increases of .7% and .6% at Post-tests 1 and 2 respectively.

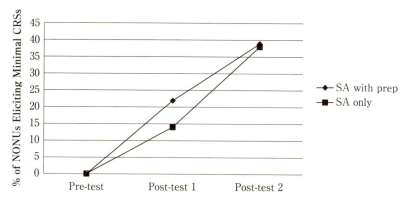

Figure 8 Comparing non-understanding situations eliciting minimal CRSs.

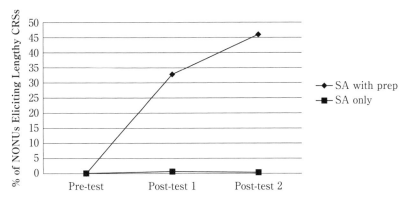

Figure 9 Comparing non-understanding situations eliciting lengthier CRSs.

Conclusion: Summary and Implications

In summarising the findings of this study, RQs 1 and 2 are revisited and answered in succession below.

RQ 1: What are the effects of short-term study abroad (SA) on the listenership of Japanese EFL university students (JEFLs)?

The findings of this study demonstrate that short-term study abroad had a positive effect on the listenership behaviour of the majority of the JEFLs in this study, irrespective of whether they had had pre-SA instruction or not. On average, members of both Groups A and B displayed improvement in several key areas, which include frequency, variability, discourse contexts, simultaneous speech, and functions.

RQ 2: What are the effects of pre-SA instruction on the listenership of JEFLs upon returning from SA?

Although both groups exhibited improvement in several areas of listenership, the findings, overall, show that Group A, the group that received pre-

SA instruction, clearly outperformed Group B, the group that did not receive pre-SA. On average, members of Group A not only improved in more of the of the sub-areas of listenership, but in the areas where both groups had improved, the gains made by members of Group A often tended to be more noticeable and sustainable over time. For instance, regarding variability, members of Groups A and B showed similar levels of improvement by sending far fewer minimal backchannels after they had studied abroad; however, the increases in the number of extended listener responses sent by Group A far outpaced that of Group B. Similarly, concerning function, both Groups A and B improved in that they sent significantly fewer unconventional listener responses while sending significantly more minimal conversational repair strategies when they did not understand; however, only Group A was able to significantly increase the number of lengthier conversational repair strategies they employed in this context over time. Further, Group A showed improvement by sending significantly fewer simultaneous speech backchannels over time, while Group B's frequency level slightly increased.

In addition, the findings of this study help shed light on what students actually gain linguistically when they study abroad. As noted previously, short-term study abroad does not seem to yield better results than stay-at-home classroom instruction where grammar, listening and reading are concerned. Rather, as the results of this study have shown, the benefits of short-term study abroad may be more evident in terms of conversational output and pragmatic competence.

Lastly, the findings of this study clearly point to the benefits of explicit pre-SA instruction. While the content of pre-SA preparation courses is likely to vary depending on institutional goals in various contexts, the researchers advocate incorporating some elements of instruction that focus on conversational features of language and pragmatic competence. To that end, the pre-SA instruction on listenership that was used in this study proved to be effective and can be explored as a potential framework for instructors moving forward. Instructors would be well-served in administering initial consciousness raising activities to draw students' attention to various features of conversation; subsequently, instructors would do well to facilitate discussions among their learners on the implications of cross-cultural communication styles (i.e. to further raise awareness and explore perceptions of various conversational behaviours across cultures); then, instructors would be wise to expose their learners to authentic models of English that demonstrate effective conversational and listenership behaviour in a host of situations, and, finally, instructors should provide learners with ample practice opportunities and offer subsequent corrective feedback. For more in-depth information about how to create and administer the specific aspects of such a course, instructors can consult the previous work of Cutrone (2016b).

Acknowledgement

This work was supported by JSPS KAKENHI Grant Number 15K02754.

References

Capper, S. (2000). Nonverbal communication and the second language learner: Some pedagogical considerations. *The Language Teacher, 24* (5), 19-23.

Cutrone, P. (2005). A case study examining backchannels in conversations between Japanese-British dyads. *Multilingua - Journal of Cross-Cultural and Interlanguage* Communication, *24* (1), 237-274.

Cutrone, P. (2010). The backchannel norms of native English speakers: A target for Japanese L2 English learners. *University of Reading Language Studies Working*

Papers, *2* (1), 28-37.

Cutrone, P. (2014). A cross-cultural examination of the backchannel behavior of Japanese and Americans: Considerations for Japanese EFL learners. *Intercultural Pragmatics 11* (1), 83-120.

Cutrone, P. (2016a). Explicit vs. implicit instruction: Investigating backchannel behavior in the Japanese EFL classroom. *Asian EFL Journal, 18* (2), 9-88.

Cutrone, P. (2016b). The explicit teaching of backchannel behavior to Japanese EFL/ESL learners. In Tatsuki, D., & D. Fujimoto (Eds.) *Back to basics: Filling in the gaps in pragmatics teaching materials* (pp. 36-48). Tokyo, Japan: The Japan Association for Language Teaching, Pragmatics Special Interest Group.

Freed, B. (1998). An overview of issues and research in language learning in a study-abroad setting. *Frontiers: The Interdisciplinary Journal of Study-abroad, 4* (1), 21-60.

LoCastro, V. (1987). Aizuchi: A Japanese conversational routine. In L. Smith (Ed.), *Discourse across cultures: Strategies in world Englishes* (pp. 101-113). London: Prentice Hall.

Maynard, S. K. (1997). Analyzing interactional management in native/non-native English conversation: A case of listener response. *IRAL, 35* (1), 37-60.

McCarthy, M. (2003). Talking back: "Small" interactional response tokens in everyday conversation. *Research on Language and Social Interaction, 36* (1), 33-63.

Sato, Y. (2008). Oral communication problems and strategies of Japanese university EFL learners. Unpublished PhD Thesis, University of Reading, Reading.

Tanaka, K., & Ellis, R. (2003). Study-abroad, language proficiency, and learner beliefs about language learning. *JALT Journal, 25* (1), 63-84.

White, S. (1989). Backchannels across cultures: A study of Americans and Japanese. *Language in Society, 18* (1), 59-76.

Part 2: Teaching and Production of Pragmatics in Academic Writing: Seeking the Relation to Speaking

Differences in the Quality of Interaction between Spoken and Written Communication

Misa Fujio

Abstract

Interaction is one of the most important features of oral communication. In Chafe (1982), fragmentation and attachment, that result from interaction, are regarded as the main important characteristics of spoken discourse, which is in contrast to integration and detachment that are features of written discourse in which the writer and the reader are physically detached. Even in written communication, however, interaction will be observed if we see the process of communication in terms of how the publication is read, interpreted, and even consumed and disseminated. At the same time, the interactive aspects of spoken language should be more carefully discussed, according to the type of interaction, such as a dyad conversation or a group discussion. In this chapter, the quality of interaction both in spoken and written communication will be revisited and some suggestions will be made for future English education in Japan.

Keywords: interaction, spoken discourse, written discourse, collaborative theory

Introduction

For the past decade, the terms such as *globalization* or *global human resources* have been drawing ever increasing attention in Japan. In fact, in 2012, the Ministry of Education, Culture, Sports, Science and Technology (MEXT) issued a report listing the qualifications needed for global human resources. It consisted of three major categories: 1) language ability and communicative competence, 2) being proactive, challenging, cooperative, flexible, and having responsibility and a mission; and 3) ability to understand different cultures as well as retaining a Japanese identity (MEXT, 2012). This implies that, in order to become a global human resource or a globally-minded leader, the ability to interact with people from different cultures and to understand different cultures, in most cases using English, will be indispensable.

In terms of interaction, the author has been mainly investigating spoken discourse, especially between native speakers and non-native speakers of English in both academic contexts (e.g., Fujio, 2011, 2013, 2014a) and in professional contexts (e.g. Fujio, 2004, 2014b, 2018a).

However, a summer seminar at the London School of Economics and Political Science (LSE, 2017) prompted her to change her viewpoint of interaction and to realize that written communication is also a more interactive process than usually considered when taken as a process of production, interpretation, consumption and dissemination.

In addition, the quality of interaction in spoken language varies from type to type: from a dyad face-to-face conversation, a group discussion in an academic situation, to a business meeting in which internal power relations are also integrated.

Therefore, in this chapter, the author will look into the quality of interaction both in spoken and written communication and identify the similarities and differences.

In the next section, theoretical frameworks about interaction and different types of interaction centered on oral communication will be reviewed. Then, in the following section, interaction in written documents will be investigated, which will be followed by the discussion about the differences in interaction between spoken and written communication. In the last section, the author will propose several suggestions for future English education in Japan, based on the findings from the previous sections. Finally, the limitations of the current study and future research agenda will be summarized in the section of Conclusion.

Literature Review

In this section, several of the most influential theories about the quality of spoken and written communication and interactional mechanism will be summarized.

Spoken and Written Communication

Distinctive linguistic features in spoken and written discourse are extensively discussed by Chafe (1982). She measured linguistic features in spoken and written discourse and revealed visible differences between the two. Spoken discourse includes much more first person references, emphatic particles, and fuzziness while written discourse uses more relative clauses, sequences of prepositional phrases or complement clauses. She discussed these differences in two axes, structure and attachment, which is summarized by the author in Table 1.

Table 1
Features of Spoken and Written Discourse

	Spoken	Written
Structure	Fragmentation	Integration
Attachment	Involvement	Detachment

The differences clearly indicate that, in spoken communication in which speed and emotional attachment are the most important, the utterance tends to be rather fragmentary, which can be completed by the interlocutor, and through which togetherness or emotional attachment are even strengthened.

On the other hand, in written communication, in which the writer and the reader are physically detached, more detailed information tends to be included as represented by more use of relative clauses. In addition, expressions showing some distance between the writer and the audience are also observed, such as more frequent use of passive forms.

The differences between spoken and written language are also elaborated by Clark and Brennan (1991) in terms of the constraints in communication and the costs (time and effort) paid by the communicators. They discussed eight different constraints and eleven costs paid in communication of two-way personal media, including face-to-face conversation (FTF hereafter), telephone, video teleconference (VT), email and personal letters. In Table 2, the author summarized the list of eight constraints which different media may impose on communication (terminal teleconference and answering machines were excluded in this table because of the fact they are much less frequently used now).

As Table 2 indicates, because of the above constraints, the communica-

Table 2
Eight Different Constraints in Two-Way Communication

Constraints	Description	Related Media
Copresence	A and B share the same physical environment	FTF
Visibility	A and B are visible to each other	FTF, VT
Audibility	A and B communicate by speaking	FTF, Telephone, VT
Contemporality	B receives at roughly the same time as A produces	FTF, Telephone, VT
Simultaneity	A and B can send and receive at once and simultaneously	FTF, Telephone, VT
Sequentiality	A's and B's turns cannot get out of sequence	FTF, Telephone, VT
Reviewability	B can review A's messages	email, letters
Revisability	A can revise messages for B	email, letters

tors have to adjust their costs to pay for each media. For example, since FTF communication includes contemporality, simultaneity, and sequentiality (in other words, speed to respond is the most important), the speaker cannot therefore afford the high formulation costs, which is the time and effort to formulate complicated utterances. In Table 3, the author summarized the 11 costs to pay in communication and who is required to pay the costs.

The first two, Formulation and Production Costs, are to be paid by the addresser and the next two, Reception and Understanding, are by the addressee. Then, all the rest are to be paid by both the addresser and the addressee. For example, in the Start-up Cost, not only the addresser but also the addressee must notice that the addresser has uttered something and accept it.

Table 3
Eleven Different Costs in Two-Way Communication

Costs	Description	Person to pay
Formulation	Costs to formulate and reformulate utterances	Addresser
Production	Costs to produce utterances	Addresser
Reception	Costs to receive or wait utterances	Addressee
Understanding	Costs to understand utterances	Addressee
Start-up	Costs of starting up a new discourse	Both (of addresser and addressee)
Delay	Costs of delaying an utterance to plan, revise, and execute it more carefully	Both
Asynchrony	Costs to time utterances with great precision (for example, begin an utterance at the completion of the prior speaker)	Both
Speaker change	Costs of changing speakers	Both
Display	Costs to display to show they are attending (for example, nodding or gazing)	Both
Fault	Costs associated with producing an utterance fault, such as mistake or missaying	Both
Repair	Costs to repair the utterance	Both

As in the case of the constraints mentioned before, all the above costs vary from medium to medium. For example, display costs are minimized in FTF communication, slightly higher in video conference, and much higher in email. In particular, formulation costs, delay costs, fault costs, and repair costs demonstrate the differences between spoken and written communication. The formulation and delay costs are usually minimized in FTF communication in which a timely response should be prioritized while these two costs tend to become higher in written communication in order to formulate more precise messages. Likewise, fault and repair costs are by far the most significant in written medium such as emails or letters, in which correcting any misunderstanding takes much more time and effort, and sometimes the misunderstanding might develop into a more serious consequence.

Thus, taking inappropriate costs may result in unsuccessful communication and might be fatal in some occasions.

For example, Fujio (2011) introduced a longitudinal case in which a Japanese graduate student took high formulation and delay costs in conversations with a native speaker of English (who was her monthly conversational partner in the research) and her speaking speed did not improve much over a year, which resulted in her becoming a rather passive listener in their conversations.

This point, how to communicate according to the media, will be revisited in the last section as suggestions for future English education in Japan.

Mechanism of Interaction

Next let's turn our eyes to the mechanism of interaction in FTF conversation.

Interaction in conversation has been discussed in several different ways. The most influential examples include the cooperative principle (Grice, 1975) or the Principles of Quantity and Relation (Levinson, 1987). Here, the collaborative theory (Wilkes-Gibbs, 1997) will be introduced, since, based on the theory, we can observe communication both in terms of the equality of contribution and the efficiency and economy of communication.

In this theory, conversation in any language is considered as a collaborative process of discovering and extending "the boundaries of common ground" of both participants or of "coordinating individual beliefs into mutual ones." This process is called the "grounding process," consisting of the basic unit called "contribution", that is, an action or utterance to update their common ground.

Conceptually, the grounding process is divided into a "presentation phase" and an "acceptance phase." In the presentation phase, "Speaker A presents an utterance for B to consider", and in the acceptance phase, Speaker A and B "try to establish that they have a satisfactory mutual interpretation of the action" (Wilkes-Gibbs, 1997, p. 240).

In the acceptance phase, Speaker B indicates either a positive evidence showing B's understanding or a negative evidence showing his/her non-understanding. In the case of negative evidence, the original message will be refashioned until both A and B reach an understanding. The below are examples of the two cases.

1) Present 1:   A: Did you go to the store?
    Accept 1/Present 2:   B: Yes. I got the milk.

2) Present 1:   A: Did you go to the store?
    Present 2:   B: Excuse me?
    Accept 2/Present 3:   A: Did you go to the grocery store this morning?
    Accept 3, 1/Present 4:   B: Yes. I got the milk.

There are two major principles that regulate conversations: the principle of mutual responsibility and the principle of least collaboration effort. The first principle deals with balance in contribution that "the participants share responsibilities for trying to solve [a basic coordination problem] to their collective satisfaction" while the second principle considers the aspect of labor in communication and that "the participants try to minimize the work they both do collectively" (Wilkes-Gibbs, 1997, p. 241). This second principle has been discussed under several different names as the Cooperative Principle (Grice, 1975), the Principles of Clarity and Economy (Poulisse, 1997), the Principles of Quantity and Relation (Levinson, 1987), or the principle of least collaboration effort (Clark & Wilkes-Gibbs, 1986; Clark & Brennan, 1991). These principles indicate that the process of communication or interaction will be a more economical and energy-saving than is usually believed.

Based on the above principles, successful communication will be described in terms of the two aspects: "flawless presentations and trouble-free acceptances" (Clark & Brennan, 1991) (based on the principle of least collaboration effort) and more balanced contributions between the participants (based on the principle of mutual responsibility). Fujio (2011), based on the collaborative theory, defined successful communication more specifically. The four aspects to judge successful communication are "1) how few breakdowns there are, 2) if there are any, how quickly the breakdown is overcome, 3) how clearly and effectively an acceptance is made (and how little presentation is extended because of an improper sign of acceptance) and 4) how balanced the contributions of the two interlocutors are" (p. 55).

In communication, basically, both Speaker A and Speaker B alternately provide a contribution, and then an acceptance phase also functions as a presentation. However, in a native speaker and a non-native speaker (NS-NNS) dyad, there is a tendency for the NS to ask (present) a question and for the NNS only to answer (accept) it without any additional information

(Long, 1983). In that case, the NS has more burden and the resources of both participants are not exploited maximally, which violates the principle of mutual responsibility and, as a result, does not meet the criteria for successful communication as explained above.

In L2 communication, therefore, language education should focus on not only accuracy in production, but also how to contribute to the conversation. Especially, speaking up and making a contribution in a group discussion is by far more difficult than a dyad conversation. In the next section, a more complicated turn-taking behaviour in a group discussion will be discussed.

Turn-Taking in a Group Discussion

The research in turn-taking was pioneered by Sacks, Schegloff, and Jefferson (1974), in which turn-taking was considered as "the distribution of talk among the parties" or "the sequences in which the talk shifted from one to another or was retained by a single party" (p. 697). They named the earliest possible point at which the speaker can change a "transition-relevance place (TRP)" and presented the basic rules for turn-taking at the initial TRP as follows:

1) if the "current speaker selects next" technique is used, then "the party so selected has the right and is obliged to take next turn to speak";
2) if the technique is not involved, then "self-selection for next speakership" may be instituted;
3) if the 2) above does not work, the current speaker may continue "unless another self-selects" (p. 704).

However, turn-taking in actual communication is not as easy as regulated, because it is very context-sensitive even though regulated by context-free rules.

In intercultural communication, in particular, linguistic ability strongly affects turn-taking behaviors. For example, Long (1981) disclosed that, in NS-NNS interaction, the mean number of topic-continuing moves per topic initiation is significantly lower and the proportion of topic-initiating moves utilizing a question is significantly higher. It indicates, as touched upon in the previous section, a native speaker usually leads the conversation, initiating questions, and topics more frequently change than in an NS-NS dyad.

In a group discussion, turn-taking becomes even more complicated because more variables are incorporated: language ability, expertise, personal characters, and the group dynamism. For example, Fujio (2018b) revealed that her participants (five Japanese university students who studied in the UK for a year) reiterated their difficulty in speaking up in group discussions although they realized their improvement in daily conversation. Their hesitation in speaking up in a group discussion is partly due to their linguistic constraints, partly lack of expertise in academic topics, and their less active attitude in developing their own ideas (which might be partly caused by the rather passive learning style at Japanese universities).

With regard to turn-taking, there are also several interesting studies in the professional contexts, especially, in business.

The first line of those studies is cultural tendencies. Yamada (1990) revealed that the turn-taking of Japanese participants were less active than American counterparts in their in-house business meetings. Likewise, Gudykunst and Nishida (1994) indicated that turns are distributed relatively equally in collective cultures including Japan, while they tend to be distributed unevenly in individualistic cultures.

There are several studies, however, disclosing different turn-taking styles even among Asian countries. Du-Babcock and Tanaka (2010) revealed, focusing on the turns showing disagreement, that Hong Kong Chinese participants showed disagreement more visibly than Japanese counterparts who used interrogative forms to avoid direct confrontation. Du-Babcock (1999, 2006) reported different turn-taking styles of the same participants by media, based on several meeting data of Hong Kong bilinguals. They used a spiral topic management style in their first language (Cantonese) while using a linear one in their second language (English).

Another line of study has disclosed that the internal status of an organization influences turn-taking style and even non-native speakers of English (Japanese managers) took turns more aggressively than native speakers. In Miller (1994) or Fujio (2004), Japanese managers rather took a direct approach to show disagreement toward their counterparts, which is rather opposite from the indirect ways typically reported as the Japanese style.

Thus, in professional fields like business, different dynamics may work for turn-taking, other than linguistic ability, partly because turn-taking style and power relations influence each other and less frequent turn-taking may disempower the participants (Tanaka, 2008).

The relationship between turn-taking and power is an especially interesting topic in interaction and also an important agenda for future English education in Japan. Therefore, this topic will be further discussed in the last section.

Interaction in Written Communication

This section will focus on interaction in written communication.
As reviewed in Section 1, in the case of written communication, the writ-

er and the reader are physically detached and cannot interact directly as in the case of spoken communication. Then, are there no interactions in written communication?

Previous studies in written communication, particularly in documents, have focused on the content itself and the process of the documents being produced and used have rather left unexamined. The significance of the document, however, lies in the "dynamics of reading and writing" as pointed out by Freeman and Maybin (2011). Although they discussed the dynamics of documents in the political context, their basic notion can be applied to any type of written communication.

> The social and political significance of the document inheres in the dynamics of reading and writing, in the essential activity of writing and the relative passivity of reading, or at least in our constructs of them. We think of the writer as source or origin of what is written, of the reader as recipient of something given. While the reader 'follow' the text, autonomy lies with the writer. In this way, authority appears to be based on, produced by, authorship. At the same time, however, the document disaggregates acts of communication, separating the sender and receiver of a message in time and space. It extends the scope and reach of command, making it possible to direct action over time and at a distance. (Freeman & Maybin, 2011, p. 156)

Their discussion signifies three important points. First of all, although written communication, as represented by documents, seems to be one-way communication, it is a dynamic and interactive process between the writer and reader. Although the reader seems to be a passive receiver of messages, s/he can disseminate it as an active agent, sometimes adding and creating his/her original message. Second, the message sent by the writer can be transmitted and communicated over time and at a distance. Therefore, the original writing can be read and interpreted in a very different way, using the specific context of the time and place the reader resides. For example, when a publication of feminism (e.g. Feminine Mystique by Friedan) was read in 1960s and 1970s, it was a book to enlighten women. Now it is a publication including the history that has significantly influenced the feminism movement we have already developed and has different impacts on us. So, the meaning of a publication is actually decided by the reader. Third, unlike oral communication in which the speaker usually knows whom they speak to, written communication is "directed at an unknown reader" and addressed in general terms. This means that, since the author cannot gauge how much knowledge and context s/he can share with the reader, the interpretation totally depends on the receiver's side, more than the case of spoken communication. Therefore, when we shed light on how the readers consume the original text (not just how the writers produce it), in other words, how the readers understand, interpret, and even disseminate the original message, written communication becomes a very dynamic, flexible, and interactive one.

Suggestions for Future English Education in Japan

In the last section of this chapter, the author would like to make some suggestions for future English education in Japan, with a focus on three points: education based on register, education incorporating turn-taking, and raising awareness of the active and interactive role of the reader.

Teaching with a Focus in Register

Partly because the English education in Japan has focused on grammar-translation, still many Japanese learners of English experience some fear of making grammatical mistakes.

However, when we consider the differences between spoken and written discourse discussed in the previous sections, it is rather natural and normal to produce incomplete sentences in oral communication. Instead of focusing on the preciseness of the meaning, we should pay more attention to (the role of) the interlocutor(s) and how to co-construct discourse and realize the fact that oral communication is to be established by both the speaker and the interlocutor. In other words, it should be taught that we minimize formulation or delay costs in oral communication in order to give a timely response to the interlocutor, while we minimize fault or repair costs in written language and therefore we make more precise and integrated sentences.

If the Japanese education can incorporate these differences in register into the classroom (in particular, differences between spoken and written language, and between formal and informal language), it will make Japanese learners of English aware of the tolerance of grammatical mistakes in oral communication and encourage them to speak up in English. At the same time, they will be more sensitive to the differences in expressions between spoken and written language and among different media in written discourse such as traditional letters, e-mail correspondence, and SNS. It will be especially useful for them to realize the differences in the selection of vocabulary and politeness by media and to adjust their communication style accordingly.

Teaching with a Focus on Turn-Taking

The author's previous studies have disclosed that determining how to take turn is especially difficult for Japanese both in the academic context (e.g., Fujio, 2018b) and in the professional context (e.g., Fujio, 2008). The difficulties vary from selecting and initiating a topic to attract the interlocutor in a small talk, to speaking up in a group discussion or disagreeing in a professional meeting. The findings indicate several different facets we may pay attention to in our future English education.

In order to select a topic interesting to the interlocutor, perhaps we will need more knowledge about other countries. If we are familiar with the culture or the society of the interlocutors, we can not only select interesting topics to the interlocutors but also more easily identify our common ground and decide how to explain the topics. For example, when we explain culturally specific topics such as the Japanese New Year's Day or Japanese hierarchical society, we can compare cultural differences with those of the interlocutors and take specific examples. In this sense, combining our English education with intercultural education should be more emphasized.

Next, teaching the manner of turn-taking itself may be beneficial. Several studies have revealed that Japanese participants tend to disagree indirectly or to avoid disagreement until the very end (e.g. Du-Bacock & Tanaka, 2010; Fujio & Tanaka, 2012). However, in discussions in English, we are expected to present our disagreement more clearly. Therefore, how to show disagreement in English should be incorporated in English education, including specific expressions such as "I have a slightly different perspective" as an example of mild disagreement or "I cannot see your point" as one of rather strong disagreement. As Tanaka (2008) reported, we always have to be aware that fewer turn-taking makes us even less powerful speakers in intercultural communication in English.

Teaching with a Focus on the Active and Interactive Role of the Reader

As discussed in the section of the interaction in written communication, the role of the reader is much more active and interactive than usually assumed. This is basically the same for the role of the listener, who has to be engaged in conversation using a wide variety of positive evidence or reactive tokens. In the case of reading, however, the degree of being an active communicator is even more significant, because reading itself is a very active process and we cannot appreciate even a single line unless we try to read it. It is the reader who starts the act of reading, who interprets the message, using his/her own background knowledge, and who even disseminates the message to others.

It is revealed by the TOEIC official site (IIBC, 2019) that the average score of reading part is much lower than that of listening and it is harder to enhance this score. Therefore, it is the skill that is most challenging to improve upon and at the same time it is the skill with the greatest potential to improve one's writing skills, needless to say speaking skills. If we teach this active role of reading, we may introduce the excitement of reading to the learners of English.

Conclusion

In this chapter, the author discussed the basic mechanism of interaction and various interactive features of spoken and written communication. Then, based on these features, the author made some suggestions for future English education in Japan: teaching with a focus on register, turn-taking, and active role of the readers, in particular. It is hoped that this chapter will, in a way or another, contribute to future empirical studies in English education in Japan and enable Japanese speakers of English to be more successful in all aspects of their communication.

References

Chafe, W. L. (1982). Integration and involvement in speaking, writing, and oral literature. In D. Tannen (Ed.), *Spoken and written language: Exploring orality and literacy*. Norwood, NJ: Ablex.

Clark, H.H., & Brennan, S. E. (1991). Grounding in communication. In L. B, Resnick, J. M. Levine, & S. D. Teasley (Eds.), *Perspectives on socially shared cognition*. Washington, DC: American Psychological Association.

Clark, H.H., & Wilkes-Gibbs, D. (1986). Referring as a collaborative process. *Cognition, 22*, 1-39.

Du-Babcock, B. (1999). Topic management and turn-taking in professional communication: First- versus second-language strategies. *Management Communication Quarterly, 12*, 544-574.

Du-Babcock, B. (2006). An analysis of topic management strategies and turn-taking behavior in Hong Kong bilingual environment: The impact of culture and language use. *Journal of Business Communication, 43*, 21-42.

Du-Babcock, B., & Tanaka, H. (2010). Turn-taking behavior and topic management strategies of Chinese and Japanese business professionals: A comparison of intercultural group communication. *Proceedings of the 75th Annual Convention of ABC (Association for Business Communication)*. Tokyo: Chuo University.

Freeman, R. & Maybin, J. (2011). Documents, practices and policy. *Evidence & Policy, 7*(2), 155-170.

Friedan, B. (1963). *The feminine mystique*. New York: W. W. Norton and Company.

Fujio, M. (2004). Silence during intercultural communication: A case study. *Corporate Communications, 9*(4), 331-339.

Fujio, M. (2008). Positive and negative effects of English communication in foreign-affiliated companies operating in Japan. *The Journal of International Business Communication Association, 67,* 61-72.

Fujio, M. (2011). *Communication strategies in action: The negotiation, establishment, and confirmation of common ground.* Tokyo: Seibido.

Fujio, M. (2013). Positive effects of short-term overseas programs on Japanese university students' English communication. *Keieironshu (Journal of Business Administration, Toyo University), 82,* 13-27.

Fujio, M. (2014a). The retention and attrition of English ability by Japanese university students with short-term overseas study experience. *Keieironshu (Journal of Business Administration, Toyo University), 84,* 25-39.

Fujio, M. (2014b). The role of linguistic ability and business expertise for turn-taking in intercultural business communication. *The GABC (Global Advances in Business Communication) Journal, 3,* 1-28 (Article 4).

Fujio, M. (2018a). Challenges facing globally-minded leaders in a Japanese-European joint venture company. *Business Communication Research and Practice (BCRP), 1*(1), 18-25.

Fujio, M. (2018b). The effects of overseas study on Japanese university students: Challenges and opportunities in the development of intercultural competence and impacts on future career. *JACET Selected Papers, 5, 50-79.*

Fujio, M. & Tanaka, H. (2012). "Harmonious disagreement" in Japanese business discourse. In J. Aritz & R. Walker (Eds.), *Discourse perspectives on organizational communication* (pp. 81-99). Maryland: Fairleigh Dickinson University Press.

Grice, H. (1975). Logic and conversation. In P. Cole, & J. Morgan (Eds.), *Syntax and semantics, 3.* New York: Academic Press.

Gudykunst, W., & Nishida, T. (1994). *Bridging Japanese/North American differences.* Thousand Oaks, CA: Sage.

IIBC (The Institute for International Business Communication) (2019). IIBC official English site. Retrieved Jan 6, 2019, from https://www.iibc-global.org/english.html

Levinson, S. (1987). Minimization and conversational inference. In J. Verschueren, & M. Bertuccelli-Papi (Eds.), *The pragmatic perspective.* Amsterdam: John Benjamins.

Long, M. (1981). Questions in foreigner talk discourse. *Language Learning, 31(1),*

137-157.

Long, M. H. (1983). Native speaker/non-native speaker conversation and the negotiation of comprehensible input. *Applied Linguistics, 4,* 126-141.

LSE (2017) Qualitative Research Methods (A programme of summer school) at The London School of Economics and Political Science.

MEXT (2012). Gurobaru jinzai ikusei senryaku no gaiyou [An overview of how to foster global human resources] Retrieved Jan 6, 2019, from http://www.mext.go. jp/b_menu/shingi/chousa/koutou/052/052_02/siryou/__icsFiles/afieldfile /2012/10/30/1327449_07.pdf

Miller, L. (1994). Japanese and American indirectness. *Journal of Asian Pacific Communication, 51* (1&2), 37-55.

Poulisse, N. (1997). Compensatory strategies and the principles of clarity and economy. In G. Kasper, & E. Kellerman (Eds.), *Communication Strategies.* New York: Addison Wesley Longman.

Sacks, H., Schegloff, E., & Jefferson, G. (1974). A simplest systematic for the organization of turn-taking for conversation. *Language, 50*(4), 696-735.

Tanaka, H. (2008). Communication strategies and cultural assumptions: An analysis of French-Japanese business meetings. In S. Tietze (Ed.), *International management and language* (pp. 154-170). New York: Routledge.

Wilkes-Gibbs, D. (1997). Studying language use as collaboration. In G. Kasper, & E. Kellerman (Eds.), *Communication strategies: Psycholinguistic and sociolinguistic perspectives.* London: Longman.

Wilkes-Gibbs, D., & Clark, H. H. (1992). Coordinating beliefs in conversations. *Journal of Memory and Language, 31,* 183-194.

Yamada, H. (1990). Topic management and turn distribution in business meetings: American versus Japanese strategies. *Text, 10,* 271-295.

Overuse of "Reason": Effect of L1 Transfer on L2 English and Japanese Writing

Megumi Okugiri

Abstract

Japanese learners overuse the word "reason(s)" when writing English essays, and in particular, create a unique prefabricated pattern, "*I have three reasons.*" A corpus analysis provided two novel findings: (1) Japanese learners produce "*reason(s)*" twice as much as English speakers, but do not produce to the same extent the equivalent word "*riyū*" in their first language (L1) Japanese; and (2) the most frequent examples were a metalinguistic use exhibiting the number of "*reason(s),*" such as, "*I have three reasons why I think so*" and "*There are three reasons.*" Bidirectional analysis examined production in the second language (L2) of the Japanese word "*riyū*" by English speakers to determine if there is English L1 transfer to L2 Japanese. The results showed learners transferred the function as a discoursal marker. A qualitative analysis of the function of "*reason(s)*" suggests that learners create a unique prefabricated pattern as a strategy to maintain coherency in L2 writing, which is also evidence of L1 transfer.

Keywords: L2 writing, function, communication strategy, corpus, L1 transfer

Introduction

The ability to write in English is increasingly important as communication and education become globalized, nevertheless the teaching of writing as a learned skill is often ignored in academic settings. This is especially true in non-English speaking countries such as Japan. While both language teachers and learners acknowledge that writing skills are crucial for academics and their future careers, the number of universities and schools conducting classes to develop such skills are still very few.

Currently, English education in non-English speaking countries is generally not oriented towards discourse or pragmatics. For instance, in Japan most English writing classes are focused on learning words and sentences, and students are lucky if the focus is on writing a paragraph. As a result, most contemporary English L2 learners are not taught actual English essay writing, and thus have difficulty expressing their ideas and opinions when writing in English. Not only L2 learners but L1 learners need to be instructed to write effective academic writing. The learning does not occur as naturalists insisted that learners acquire L2 by means of natural input (Krashen, 1991). Learners need to learn adequate register, language use, expressions and discourse to deliver in the genre.

This study aims to show through usage-based linguistic analysis that L1 results in the overuse of particular patterns in L2, which is a significant challenge for learners, particularly with particular functions of a target word or phrase. In this paper, this phenomenon is described as *function transfer*, which often results in the negative use of a lexical word or phrase in L2 when the function of the target form in L2 is not a perfect match with the equivalent form in L1.

Specifically, it investigates overuse of the word "*reason*" by Japanese learners in English essays. Overuse is reflected in unique prefabricated patterns, such as "*I have three reasons*" and "*There are three reasons.*" There are actually no grammatical problems with the patterns, and the phrases do behave as a discoursal marker to indicate that the writer will state the number of reasons after the statement. Interestingly, however, the phrase is often overused by many Japanese learners, is redundant, and results in writing that to a native English-speaking reader, appears superfluous and rudimentary in skillful discourse.

This study first describes the effect of frequency in language and related studies, then illustrates the methods utilized in this study in terms of the word *reason(s)* in English and its equivalent form *riyū* in Japanese. Next is a brief explanation of the data, the results, and a discussion exhibiting the different uses and function of "*the reason*" in English essay writing between English speakers and Japanese learners. The equivalent Japanese word and expression of *riyū* in Japanese essays by Japanese speakers is also explained to elucidate the effect of function transfer from L1.

Previous Studies

This section reviews and illustrate past studies in language users' production using a usage-based model, language patterns, and language users' cognitive organisation of a language. Such analysis often exhibits less prefabricated and more flexible patterns of a language such as relative constructions, and language users' production tendency for certain patterns. Two case studies by the author, one looking at learners' use of a less prefabricated and more flexible pattern "*I think*" and the other at the more prefabricated pattern "*for example*" by Japanese learners of English, are presented to show functional transfer from L1.

Learner production data can be examined through frequency, which is a key determinant that reflects the actual use of language by learners and the structure of their cognition toward language. Frequency reveals the nature of the learners' and acquirers' language from the perspective of a usage-based approach (Diessel, 2004; Tomasello, 2003). Utterances are defined as strings of speech used for getting things said and understood, and the strings constitute a construction that has a meaning (Lieven & Tomasello, 2008; Tomasello, 2003).

Bybee (2008) suggests that more frequent strings of speech are central patterns having stronger representations in memory for language users and serve as analogical bases for forming novel instances. The central, namely prototypical pattern should be frequent in both input and output among language users. It is frequent in input because the pattern is a central pattern in the language, and the central pattern is also frequent in output because it represents the cognitive organisation of a language in addressers (Bybee & Hopper, 2001; Nattinger & DeCarrico, 1992). Bybee (2008) further explains that when a language has several phrases that are similar in semantics, and when a specific form is more frequent than others, the most frequent pattern is the central form. Language users experience both frequent and infrequent patterns of language use, and they categorise them at varying degrees of abstractness as central and non-central. The present study postulates that if a specific pattern is more frequent than other patterns for L2 learners, the more frequent type is considered to be more central compared to the other types in the learners' interlanguage (Taylor, 1995, 2008).

Continuing with this line of thought, Fox and Thompson (1990) advocate the importance of considering high frequency patterns as elements stored in a speaker's cognitive knowledge, and these patterns are at the center of a wide range of patterning that exists radially in a family-resemblance relationship. Diessel (2008, 2009) calls this concept *similarity*. It therefore seems reasonable to assume that several patterns are present in L2 learner interlanguages, and the most frequent pattern is central, and less frequent patterns, namely the peripheral constructions, are radially placed around this pattern (Lakoff, 1990; Taylor, 1995). The frequent patterns constitute language users' cognitive language, which exhibit discourse properties with pragmatic functions playing a crucial role in discourse.

Language patterns deliver a certain meaning and have a certain function for language users. Hakuta (1974) also demonstrated that in children, language use of a prefabricated pattern delivers pragmatic meanings during language acquisition. He examined the L2 English utterances of a five-year-old Japanese girl over a period of 15 months and found prefabricated patterns produced by the girl. For instance, she employed *"Do you?"* as a question marker, which was used both correctly, as in *"Do you have coffee?"* and also incorrectly, such as with, *"What do you doing, this boy?"* rather than, *"What is this boy doing?"* His analysis suggests that language acquirers produce a pattern in order to deliver a certain pragmatic meaning. This study also postulates that learner production of prefabricated patterns is not incidental, but purposeful with the aim of accomplishing pragmatic functions.

Language utilizes patterns, and they are different in degrees of frequency. In language acquisition, Nattinger and DeCarrico (1992) argue that linguistic patterns act as a crucial component of language learning and that output patterns reflect cognitive linguistic knowledge. They advanced four general types of categorisations for patterns that language may exhibit:

Polywords, Institutionalised Expressions, Phrasal Constraints and *Sentence Builders*. Polywords are short phrases that function like individual items, e.g., *by the way*. Institutionalised Expressions are lexical phrases of sentence length, e.g., *How do you do?* Phrasal Constraints are short- to medium-length phrases that are more flexible (less prefabricated) compared to Polywords, e.g., *a year ago*. And Sentence Builders are lexical phrases that provide a framework for whole sentences, where language users slot in noun phrases or verbs into the patterns, e.g., *I think (that) X*.

Diessel and Tomasello (2000) examined children's language use and revealed that the production of relative constructions produced by children was greatly affected by function in discourse. Studies in relative construction, and an example of Sentence Builders, which is a more flexible pattern of a language, reveal the cognitive organization of language users. The study examined acquisition in terms of frequency of use in the speech of four children at different stages of acquisition and found that the children first produced amalgam constructions. This construction includes no relative pronoun, as illustrated in the following example (Diessel & Tomasello, 2000, p. 139):

(1) That's doggy turn around.

Diessel and Tomasello (ibid) put forward a pragmatic explanation for the order of children's acquisition, i.e., the function is to draw attention on a referent that is perceptually present in a here-and-now context. For instance, children try to draw their caretaker's attention to a referent when they are playing with toys. Their study showed that children creatively produce a construction to denote a certain pragmatic interpretation, which reflects how language forms to carry a pragmatic function in general communicative use.

Kidd, Brandt, Lieven, and Tomasello (2007) did a usage-based study in child L1 acquisition of German relative construction and found that both German and English children used relative constructions according to input in each language. A corpus study by Reali and Christiansen (2007) also supported the results of a usage-based account and underpinned the concept that language use is a reflection of a user's cognitive organisation of the language.

Looking at the cognitive load of language users and language pattern frequency, Nation (2001) suggests that prefabricated patterns in language have the advantage of reducing processing time in general discourse, since a prefabricated pattern is seen as a unit; thus, an addresser has no need to pay close attention to every noun phrase. Nation further argues that high-frequency prefabricated patterns, i.e., idioms such as, "*Please make yourself at home* or *Have a nice day!*" are stored separately, and thus prefabricated patterns reduce processing time. Therefore, a more flexible pattern requires a greater cognitive processing load.

Okugiri, Ijuin, and Komori (2017a) examined the frequency of a more flexible pattern in L1 and L2 by investigating L2 English and L2 Japanese essay writing in comparison with the learners' L1 to elucidate the effect of L1 transfer. The usage-based analysis examined the use of "*I think*" in L2 English opinion essays at the university level. Specifically, the study found that Japanese students have a strong tendency to produce "*I think*" to mark their thesis statement, a use that is inappropriate according to typical English writing standards. Highland (2002) and Ishikawa (2009, 2012) also found overuse by Japanese learners of English, but they did not explain the condition where learners overuse the form, since it was not the focus of their study. Overuse often results in uncertainty and obscurity in essays, marring the content of the essay and leaving a negative impression on readers. The Okugiri et al. study suggested that L2 overuse is due to L1 transfer from the Japanese equivalent phrase of "*to-omou/to-kangaeru*," (both literally translated as *I think*), which are phrases frequently used in formal Japanese writing to state the thesis. Analysis of the functions of "*I think*" and "*to-omou*" and "*to-kangaeru*" were done from a usage-based account and discoursal point of view. Samples were collected from a multilingual written corpus, *The Corpus of Multilingual Opinion Essays by College Students* (Okugiri, Ijuin, & Komori, 2015).

Further, a rhetorical analysis showed different functions in the use of "*I think*" between learners and native speakers. In L2 English, Japanese learners showed a strong tendency to use "*I think*" to emphasise or mark the following sentence as their main argument or thesis as (2), meanwhile English speakers use this only to explain a personal experience or to indicate uncertain information or the writer's mere conjecture as shown in example (3):

> (2) I think newspapers and magazines are needed even if the Internet is convenient.
> (learner)
>
> (3) ... and I think my preference stems from my childhood. (English speaker)

"*I think*" functions to make some content vague or indirect, which is often appropriate in verbal exchanges. Tomasello (2000) also argue that in L1 English children use "*I think*" as a prefabricated pattern meaning "*maybe*" in their speech. On the other hand, a writer typically wants to be clear, and therefore should avoid this phrase in English essays. However, that is opposite to the use of "*to-omou*" and "*to-kangaeru*" in Japanese academic essays. In fact, "*to-kangaeru*" in particular, is preferable in Japanese essays because it implies a writer's cognitive process and a deeper consideration or judgment as a stronger statement. The following is an example by a Japanese speaker.

(4) ijyō-no   riyū-kara   watashi-wa kon'nichi-nioite-mo
above-GEN reason-ABL I-SUB   today-TEMP-also
nao hituyō-dearu   *to-kangaeru*
newspaper and magazine-SUB still necessary-ASSERTIVE think
"From the above reasons, I think we will still need newspapers and magazines even today." (Japanese speaker)

The overuse suggests the possible transfer of *to-omou* and *to-kangaeru* from Japanese. Interestingly, the functions of *I think* and *to-omou/to-kangaeru* are not a perfect match, and the Japanese learners of English showed a strong tendency to produce a different function of *I think*. Furthermore, overuse is argued as attributed to the functional gap between English *I think* and Japanese *to-omou/to-kangaeru*, even though they are described as equivalent in various dictionaries (O-lex English-Japanese Dictionary, 2013). In English L1, *I think* functions to express more personalised and indirect statement that is less than necessary in opinion essays. Meanwhile in Japanese *to-omou/to-kangaeru* function to present a writer's clear and direct opinion, and thus is frequently used in formal Japanese opinion essays. The findings suggested that Japanese learners hypothesise the linguistic form of L2 in a manner similar to that of its equivalent L1 expression without noticing the functional gap.

In a second study, Okugiri, Ijuin, and Komori (2017b) examined Japanese learner overuse of *"for example"* in English essay writing. The phrase is a fixed and nonflexible form, i.e., a polyword in terms described by Nattinger and DeCarrico (1992). This compares to a more flexible form like *"I think,"* where we suggest that Japanese learners overuse *"for example"* due to the learner's transfer of the function from the Japanese equivalent phrase *"tatoeba."* Meanwhile in English, *"for example"* is principally used to introduce an illustrative instance demonstrating a stereotypical model. In Japanese, however, *"tatoeba"* exhibits two major functions: to exhibit an illustrative instance or to show a hypothetical instance. Furthermore, Okugiri et al. (ibid) showed how Japanese learners use a hypothetical instance in L2 English that was often accompanied by a first-person pronoun *I* in order to exhibit and share their personal view or feeling. It is possible that the learners even at an advanced level use the subjective view with an intent to be convincing to the reader, although this is eventually not successful.

Another explanation Okugiri et al. (ibid) offered was the influence of dictionaries, which is one of the most accessible and likely inputs to English education in Japan. In L1 English the function of *"for example"* is fundamentally just an illustrative instance demonstrating a typical example (Oxford Dictionary of English, 2010; The American Heritage Dictionary of the English Language, 2011). Meanwhile in L1 Japanese, there are three functions for *"tatoeba"*: showing an illustrative instance and hypothetical instances as examples (5)-(6), and metaphorical instance as in "metaphorically speaking," or "so to speak" (Gendai Fukushi Yōhō Jiten, 1994; Seisen-ban Nihon Kokugo Daijiten, 2005; Meikyō Kokugo Jiten, 2010).

(5) Illustrative (L1 Japanese)

Sore wa motomoto   ryōsha ga dōiu mokuteki ni tekishite iru noka
that-SUB[5] fundamentally both-SUB what purpose for adequate be or not
nimo   kankei shite iru. Tatoeba   intānetto wa shasin   dōga   moji
also   related to   be   for example internet-SUB pictures movie words
nado no jyōhō o   tairyō   ni shunji   ni   sekaijyū ni
etc. of information-ACC[6] large amount in a moment at all the world-LOC[7]
hasshin dekiru.
send   capable

"That is also related to the adequacy of the role both media play. For example, one can send a large amount of information such as pictures, movies, words instantly to the world."

(6) Hypothetical (L1 Japanese)

Jibun no handan   niyori shiritai   jyōhō   nomi sika minai-koto
self of judgment by   want to know   information only only not to see
no-hō-ga ōi   desyō. Tatoeba   aru   websaito ni   ikutsuka no
than   frequent may for example certain website-DAT some   of
nyūsu no   komidashi ga   aru to   shimasu.
news-GEN[8] subheadings-SUB is that   assuming

"More people seem to be reading news that interests themselves. For example, assume that we have some subheadings of news on a certain website."

In English-Japanese dictionaries (Shōgakkan Random House English-Japanese Dictionary, 1993; Kenkyūsha Shin Eiwa Dai-Jiten, 2002; O-Lex English-Japanese Dictionary, 2013), *"for example"* is merely translated as *"tatoeba"* in Japanese without any functional explanation. Thus, while *"for example*" in English is used to illustrate a typical instance, English-Japanese dictionaries show nothing more than the single translation to "*tatoeba*," without sufficient explanations regarding differences in function and usage.

These studies (Okugiri et al., 2017a, 2017b) show how Japanese learners will typically acquire and utilize a unique combination of form and function in L2 English because of L1 transfer. Simply stated, Japanese learners tend to transfer the function of an L1 linguistic form to L2 even though the function is not present in the L2.

Since the studies by Okugiri et al. (2017a, 2017b) were on phrases, the relatively flexible phrase "*I think*" and fixed phrase "*for example*," for the purposes of the studies illustrated that learners have a strong tendency to produce a unique prefabricated pattern such as "*I have three reasons why I think so*," while native English speakers tend to just use the actual *reason(s)* when they show a cause, explanation, or justification for an action or event, such as writing, "*This essay will argue how the move to online reading will be mainly spurred by convenience, environmental reasons, and cost.*" This example also explains how the learners' pattern is due to functional transfer from L1. Furthermore, this points to a possible cause of overuse and implications for L2 writing instruction.

Method

The data used in the current study comes from the *Corpus of Multilingual Opinion Essays by College Students* (Okugiri, Ijuin, & Komori, 2015, hereafter MOECS). The corpus is a collection of opinion essays by college students in English and Japanese as L1 and L2 and has also been used in my previous studies (Okugiri, et al., 2017a, 2017b). The corpus includes essays of English, Japanese, Korean, and Taiwanese L1, and English of Japanese learners, Japanese of English learners, Japanese of Korean learners, and Japanese of Taiwanese learners[3]. Table 1 illustrates the type of language and the number of files available in the corpus.

The current study uses English and Japanese L1 and L2 data. The L1 and L2 English data and L2 Japanese by English learners were collected from August 2014 to August 2015, and the remaining files were collected from June 2007 to September 2009. The participants were undergraduate or graduate students at a college. They were either a volunteer or received a reward when they completed the task. In this project, native speakers are defined as people who received an education in English in any subjects in their secondary to university/college education (their teachers used English in all subjects except for foreign language classes). The participants were asked to write an essay with the following instructions[4]:

Direction: Currently, people worldwide are able to use the Internet. Some people say that since we can read the news online, there is no need for newspapers or magazines, while others say that newspapers and magazines will still be necessary in the future. Please write your

Table 1
Number of Files in MOECS Corpus

L1 Data	L2 Data
English by native speakers of English (120 files)	English by Japanese Learners (79 files)
Japanese by native speakers of Japanese (134 files)	Japanese by English Learners (32 files) Japanese by Korean Learners (55 files) Japanese by Taiwanese Learners (57 files)

opinion about this issue.

All the MOECS essays were collected in the same manner. The participants gave their consent and received an explanation indicating that the data collection was for research in their L1. The participants were told to handwrite in front of the researchers without any references including a dictionary or other reading materials to control the writing condition and to avoid plagiarism. Our focus was on collecting pure production from the participants. The essay data was subsequently typed into a text file after collection by the researchers.

There are 79 files (participants) of L2 English by Japanese learners. The current study selected all the files and randomly selected 79 files among 120 L1 English and 134 L1 Japanese essays from the corpus. For L2 Japanese by English learners, all 32 files available from the corpus were chosen. This study compares four groups: L2 English, L2 Japanese, L1 English and L1 Japanese. All the singular forms of *"reason"* and the plural form *"reasons"* from the English files, and *"riyū"* from the Japanese files were collected with CasualConc software.

Results and Discussion

The total number of sentences not limited to *"reason(s)"* or *"riyū"* in L1 English was 1,817, 1,272 for L1 Japanese, 1,996 sentences for L2 English, and 664 for L2 Japanese. Table 2 shows the frequency of the total number of sentences in each group to illustrate the size of the data and the occurrence of *"reason(s)"* and *"riyū"* along with frequency per participant. L2 English data along with L1 English was looked at first to compare a learner's production with that of a native speaker, and then with L1 Japanese to deter-

Table 2
Frequency of Sentences and Sentences with "Reason(s)" and "Riyū" in Each Group

	Total number of sentences	reason(s)/riyū	Frequency per participant
79 English Speakers (L1 English) 79	1,817	40	0.5
79 Japanese Speakers (L1 Japanese)	1,272	48	0.6
79 Japanese Learners (L2 English)	1,996	80	1.1
32 English Learners (L2 Japanese)	664	15	0.5

mine the effect of L1 transfer. Subsequently, L2 Japanese was examined to determine English L1 transfer to L2 Japanese.

The frequency of *"reason(s)"* in L1 was 40 and 80 in L2. The occurrence of *"riyū"* in L1 was 48 and 15 in L2. Since there were 32 files for L2 Japanese, which is smaller than the other groups, frequency was calculated per participant: 0.5 times for L1 English, 0.6 for L1 Japanese, 1.1 for L2 English, and 0.5 for L2 Japanese. There was a significant difference between L1 and L2 English: $\chi^2(3)=38.990$, $p > .001$, implying that native English speaker and learner production of *"reason(s)"* was significantly different.

There was no significant difference found between L1 English and Japanese; i.e., the frequency of *"reason(s)"* in L1 English and that of *"riyū"* in L1 Japanese are similar. There was also no significant difference between L1 and L2 Japanese and between L2 Japanese and L1 English. Therefore, only the Japanese learners of English produce *"reason(s)"* significantly more frequently in L2 English, which was not the case for English learners of Japanese and their use of "*riyū*."

However, a detailed analysis in function gave different results. The detailed analysis found three types of function in the use of "*reason(s)*" and "*riyū*": Cause, Deixis, and Number. Some examples are shown below:

English *reason(s)*

(7) Cause (L1 English)

This essay will argue how the move to online reading will be mainly spurred by convenience, environmental reasons, and cost.

(8) Deixis (L1 English)

…. But, the following *reasons* make it clear why this will not be beneficial, nor work.

Firstly, people still enjoy reading paper books and newspapers.

(9) Number (L2 English)

I have three *reasons* for that.

In (7), the *reason* denotes the cause for the move to online reading. This function is named Cause in this study and functions to illustrate a cause, explanation, or justification for an action or event. This is the literal meaning of *reason* (Oxford Dictionaries, 2018). The second type is Deixis, as in (8). This functions to spot the position of the cause, explanation, or justification of an action or event. The third type is Number. This operates to imply the number of causes that the writer depicts. In (9), the writer is declaring the number of reasons, namely three reasons that follow after the statement. This sentence is at the end of the introduction section, in the first paragraph, and the three reasons follow in the body, the second to fourth paragraphs. The same phenomena are found in Japanese examples of *riyū*.

Japanese *riyū*

(10) Cause (L1 Japanese)

Kono yōna keizaiteki riyū mo aru.

This like economic reason also exist

"There is also an economic reason like this."

(11) Deixis (L1 Japanese)

Ika   ni riyū   o   noberu.

Below at reason OBJ explain

"I will explain the reasons below."

(12) Number (L2 Japanese)

Sore niwa mittsu no riyū ga aru.

That for three of reason SUB exist

"There are three reasons for that."

The occurrence of each function in each group is shown in Table 3. Figures 1-4 below illustrate the proportions of each function shown in Table 3.

Figure 1 illustrates the proportion of each function of *reason(s)* by English speakers. The most frequent occurrence was the literal meaning, namely Cause (70%), followed by Deixis (28%), then Number (2%). Meanwhile, Figure 3 shows that Japanese learners tend to produce Number the most frequently (56%), followed by Deixis (23%), and Cause (21%). Comparing this with L1 Japanese data (Figure 2), the results show a different tendency from the Japanese learners of English: Deixis (48%), Cause (29%), then Number (23%). At first glance, the results seem to demonstrate no L1 transfer.

Table 3
The Occurrence of Functions in Cause, Deixis, and Number

	Cause	Deixis	Number	Total
79 English Speakers (L1 English) 79	28 (70%)	11 (28%)	1 (3%)	40 (100%)
79 Japanese Speakers (L1 Japanese)	14 (29%)	23 (48%)	11 (23%)	48 (100%)
79 Japanese Learners (L2 English)	17 (22%)	18 (22%)	45 (57%)	80 (100%)
32 English Learners (L2 Japanese)	6 (40%)	1 (7%)	8 (53%)	15 (100%)

Observing from the other direction, for example for English speakers learning Japanese, Number is the most frequent (53%), followed by Cause (40%) and Deixis (7%). The results also differ from those of L1 English and Japanese, which seems to reveal no influence by the L1.

However, if we look at the data more carefully, both learners tend to produce Number in L2. For Japanese learners, among 45 productions of Number, there were two major prefabricated patterns with "*I have*" and "*There are*." Some examples are shown below:

(13) There are four reasons.
(14) I have three reasons.

The Japanese learners of English produced 20 cases of "*There are*" and 17 cases of "*I have*," which are 44% and 38% of Number use, respectively. Tomasello (2000) explains that in L1 speech, children at an early stage utilize a holophrase, which is a single linguistic form functioning as a whole utter-

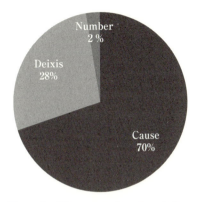

Figure 1 The proportion of each function (L1 English).

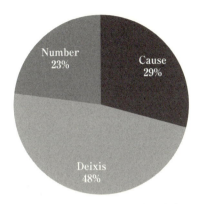

Figure 2 The proportion of each function (L1 Japanese).

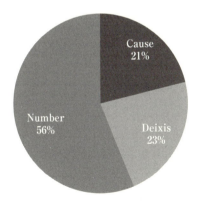

Figure 3 The proportion of each function (L2 English by Japanese learners).

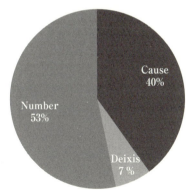

Figure 4 The proportion of each function (L2 Japanese by English learners).

ance; for instance, "*That!*" to denote "*I want that.*" A holophrase is the beginning of grammar acquisition and also indicates the language user's communicative intentions to achieve a speech act goal. If this is how a language user develops their communication strategy or language communication capability, it is possible to assume the prefabricated patterns used in (13) and (14) reflect the writer's intention to demonstrate their cognitive intention to state or to show causes or reasons to support their thesis statement. Among the 37 cases (20 cases of "*There are*" and 17 cases of "*I have*"), 35 cases are at the end of the first paragraph, right after stating the thesis statement, as in the example below:

> (15) Recently, a lot of people don't read newspapers and magazines. They read online news or get information from the Internet. Some people say that newspapers and magazines are not needed because they can watch news and get information enough from the Internet. I disagree with their opinion. I think newspapers and magazines are needed even if the Internet is convinient. *I have three reasons* for that.
>
> Firstly, we can preserve newspapers and magazines. ...
>
> (Japanese learner, errors left as in original)

In this example, the writer's statement "*I have three reasons*" for the thesis that "*newspapers and magazines are needed even if the internet is convenient*" is produced at the end of the first paragraph, and the writer then provides three reasons in the second, third and fourth paragraphs. Therefore, by stating the number of reasons, the learner writer is trying to put into the writing a function to direct readers that they can expect a description or explanation for the statement in the following paragraphs.

For the English-speaking learners of Japanese, only eight cases of Number were found among fifteen cases, and expressions varies, although two cases showed *arimasu* as shown in (16), *"that is," "There are"* in English.

(16) riyū ga ikutsumo arimasu.
　　 Reason-SUB　many　　exist
　　 "There are many reasons."

It is premature to draw a conclusion due to the small number of occurrences. But for Japanese learners, we can reasonably conclude that "*reason(s)*" for learners is a linguistic symbol functioning to announce that in the following paragraphs the writer intends to demonstrate each cause, reason, or description for the thesis statement they have just presented.

Another conclusion this study is able to draw is that both learner groups have a strong tendency to produce a Number function because the communication strategy is stated earlier, i.e., to present the writers' intention to show the cause, reason, or description of the thesis statement, and to maintain the coherence of the essay. For Japanese learners, the phrase with "*reason(s)*" is probably a discourse marker to provide readers with a clue about what the writer is going to state in later paragraphs. This may function in the same manner for English-speaking learners of Japanese.

It is also notable that the second-most frequent production for each learner group may be influenced by the L1. For Japanese learners, the Deixis function is the second-most frequent (23%), and for English-speaking learners of Japanese it is the Cause function (40%). They are in fact the most frequent functions in their L1s: Deixis (48%) for L1 Japanese and Cause (70%) for L1 English, which indicates L1 transfer; although the learner communication strategy we observed earlier, i.e., the attempt to maintain coherence is a stronger factor.

Conclusion

This study explored how native speakers of English and Japanese learners of English used the English word *"reason(s)"* in English writing. The use of the Japanese word *"riyū"* by those learning Japanese was also analyzed. Both L2 learners of English and Japanese showed a strong preference for a numbering function, which is an indication of a learners' communication strategy to maintain coherence in their writing, and an intention to give readers a clue to the structure of the essay.

In a detailed analysis of this numbering function, in L2 English, Japanese learners showed a strong tendency to use *"reason(s)"* in phrases, such as *"I have three reasons"* or *"There are three reasons,"* which functions as a discoursal marker to imply the writer's intention to state three reasons after the statement and to indicate the organization of the essay structure.

The results also revealed function transfer from L1s. The second most frequent production by Japanese learners of English was Deixis and that of English speakers of Japanese was Cause. This implies that L1 transfer was a crucial factor affecting L2 use of *"reason(s)"* and *"riyū"* after the communication strategy, which is the learners' intention to maintain coherence.

There were some limitations in this study. Although the results from the English speakers for Japanese writing contributed to the discussion, the number of files was insufficient to draw any definite conclusions. Future additional cross-linguistic studies may contribute to a better understanding of effects from L1 function transfer.

Acknowledgements

I am deeply grateful to Paul Rossiter and Lala Takeda for their tremendous support and insightful comments, and I would also like to express my gratitude to all participants and supporters of the Corpus of Multilingual Opinion Essays by College Students.

References

Bybee, J. (2008). Usage-based grammar and second language acquisition. In P. Robinson & N. Ellis (Eds.), *Handbook of cognitive linguistics and second language acquisition* (pp. 216-236). Routledge: New York.

Bybee, J., & Hopper, P. (Eds.). (2001). *Frequency and the emergence of linguistic structure*. Amsterdam: John Benjamins.

Diessel, H. (2008). The emergence of relative clauses in early child language. In *12th Biennial Rice University Symposium on Language*. Retrieved September 8, 2009, from http://www.ruf.rice.edu/~eivs/sympo/papers/Diessel.pdf

Diessel, H. (2009). On the role of frequency and similarity in the acquisition of subject and non-subject relative clauses. In T. Givon & M. Shibatani (Eds.), *Syntactic complexity* (pp. 251-276). Amsterdam: John Benjamins.

Diessel, H., & Tomasello, M. (2000). The development of relative clauses in spontaneous child speech. *Cognitive Linguistics, 11*, 131-151.

Fox, B. A., & Thompson, S. A. (1990). A discourse explanation of the grammar of relative clauses in English conversation. *Language, 66*(2), 297-316.

Hakuta, K. (1981). Grammatical description versus configurational arrangement in language acquisition: The case of relative clauses in Japanese. *Cognition, 9*(3), 197-236.

Hida, Y., & Asada, H. (1994). *Gendai Fukushi Yōhō Jiten [Comtemporary Dictionary of Japanese Adverbs]*. Tokyo: Tokyōdō Shuppan.

Hyland, K. (2002). Options of identity in academic writing. *ELT Journal* 56, 351-358.

Ishikawa, S. (2009). Phraseology overused and underused by Japanese learners of English: A contrastive interlanguage analysis. In K. Yagi & T. Kanzaki (Eds.), *Phraseology, corpus linguistics and lexicography: Papers from phraseology* (pp. 87-100). Nishinomiya, Japan: Kwansei Gakuin University Press.

Ishikawa, S. (2012). *Bēshikku kō*pasu *gengogaku [Basic corpus linguistics]*. Tokyo: Hitsuji Shobō.

Kidd, E., Brandt, S., Lieven, E., & Tomasello, M. (2007). Object relatives made easy: A cross-linguistic comparison of the constraints influencing young children's processing of relative clauses. *Language and Cognitive Processes, 22*(6), 860-897.

Kitahara, Y. (2010). *Meikyō Kokugo Jiten* (2nd ed.). Tokyo: Shōgakukan.

Krashen, S. (1994). The input hypothesis and its rivals. In N. Ellis (Ed.), *Implicit and explicit learning of languages* (pp.45-77). London: Academic Press.

Lakoff, G. (1990). *Women, fire, and dangerous things: What categories reveal about the mind.* Chicago: University of Chicago Press.

Lieven, E., & Tomasello, M. (2008). Children's first language acquisition from a usage-based perspective. In P. Robinson & N. Ellis (Eds.), *Handbook of cognitive linguistics and second language acquisition* (pp. 168-196). New York: Routledge.

Nation, I. S. P. (2001). *Learning vocabulary in another language.* Cambridge: Cambridge University Press.

Nattinger, J., & DeCarrico, J. (1992). *Language phrases and language teaching.* Oxford: Oxford University Press.

Nomura, K., Hanamoto, K., & Hayashi, R. (Eds.). (2013). *O-lex English-Japanese Dictionary* (2nd ed.). Tokyo: Ōbunsha.

Okugiri, M., Ijuin, I., & Komori, K. (2015). *The Corpus of Multilingual Opinion Essays by College Students.* Retrieved from http://www.u-sacred-heart.ac.jp/okugiri/links/moecs/moecs.html

Okugiri, M., Ijuin, I., & Komori, K. (2017a). The overuse of "I think" by Japanese learners and "to omou/to kangaeru" by English learners in essay writing. 163-168. Proceedings of Pacific Second Language Research Forum 2016.

Okugiri, M., Ijuin, I., & Komori, K. (2017b). The use of "for example" by Japanese learners of English in opinion essays. *Seishin Studies, 129*(1), 3-17.

Reali, F., & Christiansen, M. H. (2007). Processing of relative clauses is made easier by frequency of occurrence. *Journal of Memory and Language, 57*(1), 1-23.

Reason. (n.d.). Oxford Dictionaries. Retrieved from https://en.oxforddictionaries.com/definition/reason

Seisen-ban Nihon Kokugo Daijiten [*Seisen-ban Japanese Language Dictionary*]. (2005). Tokyo: Shōgakukan.

Shōgakkan Random House English-Japanese Dictionary. (1993). Tokyo: Shōgakukan.

Shōgakukan Random House Dictionary. (2006). Tokyo: Shōgakukan.

Stevenson, A. 2010. *Oxford Dictionary of English* (3rd ed.). Oxford: Oxford University Press.

Takebayashi, S. (2002). *Kenkyūsha Shin Eiwa Daijiten.* Tokyo: Kenkyūsha.

Taylor, J. R. (1995). *Linguistic categorization: Prototypes in linguistic theory* (2nd ed.). Oxford: Oxford University Press.

Taylor, J. R. (2008). Prototypes and cognitive linguistics. In P. Robinson & N. Ellis (Eds.), *Handbook of cognitive linguistics and second language acquisition* (pp. 39-65). New York: Routledge.

The American Heritage Dictionary of the English Language (5th ed.) (2011). Boston: Houghton Mifflin Harcourt. Retrieved from https://www.ahdictionary.com/word/search.html?q=for+example&submit.x=0&submit.y=0.

Tomasello, M. (2000). First steps toward a usage-based theory of language acquisition. *Cognitive Linguistics 11* (1). 61-82.

Tomasello, M. (2003). *Constructing a language: A usage-based theory of language acquisition.* Cambridge: Harvard University Press.

Notes

[1] The expected sentence is "That's the doggy that turns around."

[2] Another significant factor in the acquisition Kidd et al. found was semantic factor particularly animacy of a head noun phrase.

[3] Korean, Taiwanese and Japanese data was originally collected for *the Nihon Kankoku Taiwan-no Daigakusei-niyoru Nihongo Ikenbun Dētabēsu* (The Database of Japanese Opinion Essays by Japanese/Korean/Taiwanese University Students), by Ikuko Ijuin of Tokyo University of Foreign Studies, also downloadable from http://www.tufs.ac.jp/ts/personal/ijuin/koukai_data1.html., which was supported by Grant-in-Aid for Young Scientists (B) (Grant Number 19720119, main researcher Ikuko

Ijuin). And among 32 Japanese files of English learners, 10 files were collected by Kazuko Komori of Meiji University.

[4] The methodology originates from *the Nihon Kankoku Taiwan-no Daigakusei-niyoru Nihongo Ikenbun Dētabēsu* (The Database of Japanese Opinion Essays by Japanese/Korean/Taiwanese University Students, by Ikuko Ijuin of Tokyo University of Foreign Studies).

[5] SUB implies subjective case.

[6] ACC implies accusative case.

[7] LOC implies locative case.

[8] GEN implies genitive case.

Constructive Criticism in Talk-in-Interaction: Experienced Japanese EFL Learners' Peer-Feedback Sessions on English Essays

Ivan B. Brown and Ayaka Takeuchi

Abstract

The present study addresses the insufficient empirical basis in the literature for how experienced EFL learners in Japan might carry out constructive criticism within the sequential contexts of talk-in-interaction, with a view to the future development of instruction in L2 criticism and advice in ELT in Japan. The authors recorded, transcribed and analysed peer-feedback sessions on English essays, carried out in English by five pairs of graduate students specialising in English education at a Japanese university. Conversation analysis revealed a range of interactional and sequential practices for initiating and responding to acts of constructive, advice-focused criticism. Like other dispreferred actions, criticisms were generally carried out with dispreferred turn shapes. They could also occur in more than one sequential slot, as a first pair-part "proffer of criticism" or as a second pair-part in response to an "invitation of criticism". Some elaborate sequence-expansions were co-constructed, and noteworthy accomplishments of epistemic stance and indexing of epistemic status were observed. Pedagogical implications of this study include some difficulties encountered with dispreferred formats, suggesting potential issues in EFL learners' delivery and interpretation of interactional practices.

Keywords: conversation analysis, criticism, essay, peer-feedback, talk-in-interaction

Introduction

The actions of giving or responding to criticism or advice occur in both mundane talk (Shaw, Potter & Hepburn, 2015) and institutional settings (Waring, 2017) and members of society can be expected to employ interactional resources and practices for doing so. In EFL classroom settings, this might take place during collaborative reflections and other types of feedback sessions on various types of performance, which may involve L2 writing (Fujioka, 2013) as well as speaking (Mochizuki et al., 2012). Although such feedback is largely carried out in Japanese in many EFL classrooms in Japan, opportunities and expectations to use English may increase, in alignment with policies (e.g., MEXT, 2011, 2014) and trends towards greater use of English in the EFL classroom (Turnbull, 2018). Potentially face-threatening courses of action, such as advice, criticism or disagreement, are reported to frequently involve elaborate turn shapes (Pomerantz, 1984) and elaborate, interactionally co-constructed sequence structures (Lerner, 1996). They can therefore be challenging even for L1 speakers (Heritage & Sefi, 1992), and language learners with limited linguistic and sociocultural resources may face additional obstacles. This demands interactional competences which cannot simply be derived from the sum of speaking skills and listening skills. With a view to supporting the development of effective pedagogical approaches to doing criticism, especially for settings of giving feedback, researchers have investigated L2 speakers' actions of criticism (Fujioka, 2013; Nguyen & Basturkmen, 2010), but thus far mostly from a perspective of speech act pragmatics, with minimal attention to interactional contingencies. In this chapter, we employ principles of conversation analysis (CA) to investigate interactional practices related to constructive criticism among experienced Japanese EFL learners, introducing various alternative ways of initiating it and responding to it, and concluding with some pedagogical implications.

Background

The Guises of Criticism and the Problems of Defining Speech Acts

In speech act pragmatics, criticism has been defined as "an illocutionary act whose illocutionary point is to give negative evaluation of the hearer's (H) actions, choice, words, and products for which he or she may be held responsible. This act is performed in the hope of influencing H's future actions for H's betterment as viewed by the speaker (S) or to communicate S's dissatisfaction with or dislike regarding what H has done, but without the implicature that what H has done brings undesirable consequences to S" (Nguyen, 2008a, p. 45; cf. House & Kasper, 1981; Toplak & Katz, 2000; Tracy & Eisenberg, 1990; Wajnryb, 1995; Wierzbicka, 1987). Within this delineation and based on criticism utterances elicited from Vietnamese (L2) and Australian (L1) speakers of English, Nguyen (2008a) posited a taxonomy of criticism types under (1) direct criticism (e.g., negative evaluation, disapproval) and (2) indirect criticism (e.g., indicating standard, suggestion for change). Working with the same population, and following House and Kasper (1981) on modifications, Nguyen (2008b) employed a taxonomy of external (e.g., steers, sweeteners, disarmers, grounders) and internal modification (syntactic, lexical/phrasal).

Such definitions and taxonomies may be useful as intuitive guides for what kind of expressions are used for criticism. However, as findings from CA have shown, occurrences of criticism, advice or any other action in contexts of talk-in-interaction, may not always be neatly encapsulated in single utterances; complex sequential organizations can be involved. Moreover, social actions in interactive talk are not necessarily pre-determined; they can emerge through the moment-by-moment contingencies of interaction, in which sequential slots are at least as significant as any particular linguistic form (Sacks, 1995; Schegloff, 1999). *A priori* definitions of such things as "indirect speech acts" can thus be notoriously problematic (Levinson, 1983; Schegloff, 1988, 2007).

Conversation Analysis

Avoiding reliance on *a priori* theoretical categories or decontextualized single utterances, ethnomethodological conversation analysis (CA) takes the view that social interaction, including language use, is orderly at a minute level of detail. It thus aims to describe interactional practices in such detail, in terms of how these practices implement actions, activities, and the overall structure of conversations. Taking a radical empirical stance, analysts work with recordings of naturally occurring social interaction, supported by highly detailed and evolving transcripts, focusing on what is occurring *between* individuals, not *within* their minds. As an inductive qualitative method, CA involves repeated listening/viewing and case-by-case analysis, avoiding the constraints of theory-derived definitions, models and hypotheses (Stivers & Sidnell, 2013).

APs, Preference Organization and Type-Specific Sequences

The most basic sequence of turns within the turn-taking system elucidated by CA is the "adjacency pair" (AP) (Sacks, Schegloff, & Jefferson, 1974), which consists of a first pair-part (FPP) and, as one response among contingently relevant alternatives, a second pair-part (SPP). For example, following an assessment-FPP (expression of an opinion), either an agreement or disagreement would normally be expected as a SPP, and in most contexts, an agreement would be the preferred response, whereas a disagreement would be a dispreferred response; in other words, there is an organisation of *preference*. This is not preference in a psychological sense, but in a sequence-structural sense, as evidenced by turn-shapes and recurring sequential patterns across collections of comparable instances (Pomerantz, 1984), somewhat comparable to the concept of "markedness" in linguistics (Levinson, 1983). Preferred turn-shapes tend to involve minimal delay, minimal perturbations, and a minimal turn-constructional unit (TCU; e.g., a single word or phrase), whereas dispreferred turn-shapes tend to involve pauses, perturbations ("uh", cut-off words, etc.) and more lengthy and complex TCUs often with prefaces and accounts. As well as SPPs, FPPs can also be delivered with dispreferred turn-shapes, a practice associated with the initiation of dispreferred actions, such as complaints, criticisms, unusual requests and so on. Dispreferred FPPs are often preceded by a preliminary AP ("pre"-type sequence expansion), at which point the recipient may give a go-ahead (preferred), block the sequence (dispreferred), or pre-empt the projected action with another solution-oriented action (a pattern often classified as a pre-planned "indirect speech act" in pragmatics, hence the problems of defining this term). Although Schegloff (2007) cautions against drawing cross-paradigmatic connections between preference organization from CA, and "indirect speech acts" and types of "face" (e.g., positive vs. negative) from politeness pragmatics, there has been some noted association between preference organization and moment-by-moment actions of social (dis)alignment and (dis)affiliation (e.g., Goodwin & Heritage, 1990; Lerner, 1996). Preference is relevant to almost any type-specific sequences, which include agreement and disagreement, complaints, offering advice, giving compliments, invitations, requests and other social actions.

Criticism/Advice in Talk-in-Interaction: Conversation Analytic Studies

From a CA perspective, Don and Izadi (2013) analysed "face achieving" practices in criticism sequences among Iranian English speakers in PhD viva voce settings involving two examiner-candidate pairs. They reported that criticisms were rarely mitigated and were not prefaced by preference features, leading them to conclude that, in this context, criticisms are goal-oriented institutional actions, and interpersonal relationships might be downplayed to achieve institutional goals.

Waring (2005, 2007a, 2007b, 2012, 2017) has undertaken a long-term project on a closely related course of action, "advice", and remarks that,

> advising is characterized by its inherent asymmetries (Hutchby, 1995) that presupposes knowledge and expertise of the advice giver ([...]; Park, 2012). Such knowledge and expertise may vary from one professional (or everyday) context to the next — with different rights, roles, and constraints at play. As such, there might be a greater or lesser need for minimizing the asymmetries. [...] a persistent challenge facing the advice givers is to deliver the advice in ways that neutralize the

inherent asymmetries and thereby minimize resistance because "at stake is the advice recipient's identity claim as an engaged, discerning, independent, and competent participant" (Waring, 2007b, p. 110). This means advice can come in many shapes and forms — as information, assessments, interrogatives, and the like (Butler et al., 2010; Kinnell and Maynard, 1996; Limberg and Locher, 2012; Peräkylä and Silverman, 1991; Shaw et al., 2015; Silverman, 1997; Vehviläinen, 2012). (Waring, 2017, p. 21)

Waring's (2017) analysis of conversations between pairs of mentors and pre-service teachers in a graduate TESOL program reported *going general* practices, in which the mentors depersonalize the advice and invoke larger disciplinary or pedagogical principles to achieve alignment and professional socialisation.

This brief review suggests that a wide range of interactional practices can be involved in accomplishing criticism and advice in talk-in-interaction. The present study involved English-medium mutual peer-feedback sessions on essays among university students in Japan. In examining the participants' own orientations, we identified some courses of action which might be described variously as "criticism" and "advice", perhaps most aptly as "constructive criticism". We subsequently aimed to describe the interactional machinery (i.e., practices) deployed by these participants in collaboratively opening and accomplishing these sequences of constructive criticism. Owing to limitations of space, this chapter focuses on alternative patterns of opening and, separately, of response.

Method

This study differed somewhat from CA principles in that the participants were recruited based on their answers to an initial online survey, and their interactional setting was designed to elicit constructive criticisms. Nonetheless, their peer-feedback sessions were conducted in a non-scripted way, within a typical institutional essay-practice-and-feedback setting.

Participants

The data were collected at a university in Japan, from among ten post-graduate students specialising in English education. All of the participants selected for this study had volunteered through an open online survey within the English department, and had reported in that survey that (1) Japanese was their native language; (2) they were using English in their academic studies; (3) they had previous experience of English essay writing at institutions of higher education; and (4) they were skilled in sustaining interaction in English conversation. They were divided into five pairs, four of which were matched for year group. The aim of this design was to achieve a perspicuous interactional setting for mutual feedback through some degree of symmetry in social-academic status. These participating students were also likely to have been socialized into institutional practices for offering and receiving constructive criticism, not only on essays, but also on academic presentations, on-campus micro-teaching and school-based practice lessons.

Interactional Setting: A Peer-Feedback Session

The basic procedure and materials for the peer-feedback session followed

Nguyen's (2007) protocol; however, the instructions and time-limit for essay writing were adjusted following pilot work. Each participant chose one of five topics presented by the researchers. They were given 60 minutes to write an English essay, 10 minutes to read their partners' essays and fill in an evaluation sheet, and 15 minutes to carry out their two-way peer-feedback session, discussing their essays and evaluations in English. All of these peer-feedback interactions were video-recorded with a 360-degree camera to capture participants' verbal and non-verbal behaviours (total of 90 minutes for the whole collection) and were transcribed following CA transcription conventions (see Appendix). In consideration of the small size of the collection and limited space for reporting, we present and analyse eight excerpts mainly as singular cases, with only tentative suggestions on collection-wide practices and principles.

Analysis and Findings

Initiating Sequences of Constructive Criticism

Preliminary sequence with overt indexing of the criticism act to come

In Extract 1, N and F are discussing F's essay. Prior to this extract, N was giving a compliment to F's writing skills. As a summary, N begins a multi-TCU turn (lines 1-2) with a personalized ("I was ... ") and intensified ("really impressed") positive assessment.

Extract 1

N-F: write "do not"

```
1  N: → ((lines omitted)) >yeah yeah< I was really impressed (0.4)
2         so an:d (0.7) me- maybe if ↑I have to say ↑something.
3  F:    yes
```

```
4   N:    (0.4) ah: like critici- critic? (0.6) so like
5         [criticis]m?
6   F:    [a h : : ] to criticize?=
7   N:    =to critiꜜcize? yeah=
8   F: →  =un=
9   N:    =so: maybe, (0.4) this?((points))
10        (.)
11  N:    like (.) >maybe you< have to: write do- do not, (0.4)
```

In line 2, however, N's positive summary turns out to be a preface to a dispreferred action, with several perturbations including a pause, a trail-off ("so"), a conjunction ("and") with a sound-stretch projecting an uncertain extension to the turn, another pause and a cut-off word ("me-"). The restart ("maybe") implies a lexical downgrading of certainty, which leads into the idiomatic dangling if-clause, "if I have to say something" (with downward intonation). The ostensibly neutral "something" is contextually hearable as a euphemism, with invocation of the setting-related requirement of *having to say* a "something" which might not otherwise be said, thereby functioning as an account and a reference to the warrant for offering criticism. Right on cue, in the transition-relevance place (TRP) at the end of this turn, F gives the go-ahead pre-SPP, "yes" (line 3), to complete the pre-sequence. In lines 4-5, however, N then formulates an explicit clarification of her pre-FPP, as a syntactic extension of that pre-FPP, thereby re-calibrating it as one extended pre-FPP. This then morphs into a self-initiation of an inserted repair sequence, first through some self-repair work (as is preferred; Schegloff, Jefferson, & Sacks, 1977) with a cut-off attempt, then two try-marks (Sacks & Schegloff, 1979) to seek mutual recognition of either "critic" or "criticism", making other-repair relevant. F then responds in line 6 with a third related form, "to criticize?", as a candidate other-repair (possibly building on N's cut-off "like critici-" in line 4, but also arguably demonstrating understanding through an alternative form, rather than merely claiming understanding through a simple repeat [Sacks, 1995]).

This insertion sequence is closed with N's confirmation-repeat and acceptance (line 7) of F's candidate repair, and F gives a second go-ahead "un" (line 8) to N's preliminary to a criticism. N then seeks mutual understanding of the location of a relevant point in F's essay (points & says "this?" in line 9, followed by a micro-pause in line 10— a TRP), which could be heard as a 2nd pre-FPP to follow what might have been a "preliminary-to-preliminary" sequence ("pre-pre"; Schegloff, 2007), though there is no clear response from F. N nonetheless launches her base-FPP (line 11), again prefaced by the somewhat hesitant "like" and another micro-pause, to deliver criticism on F's use of contracted forms in a formal essay, saying "you have to write do- do not".

Although overt indexing of a prospective action commonly occurs in first position in pre-pre sequences (Schegloff, 2007), this was the only instance in this study's collection of an explicit naming of the action of criticism in a preliminary sequence. It is significant, nevertheless, to observe that (1) this explicit prospective indexing of an action was tied with an invocation of some kind of environmental or normative pressure to offer criticism, as an account and an obliquely indexed warrant to do so; (2) although N's proffer of criticism potentially ascribes her a superior epistemic stance (K+) (Heritage, 2012) relative to F, she takes a humble epistemic stance (K−) in initiating other-repair (or inviting correction; Sacks, 1995), which arguably orients to symmetrical epistemic status; and (3) the pre- and insertion sequence expansions, with immediate go-aheads and unhesitant attempts to seek and to display understanding, display intense cooperation in the achievement and maintenance of intersubjectivity.

Praise followed with "but"-prefaced indexing of a critical interrogative

Extract 2 is another example of a preliminary to a criticism, though more straightforward and yet also less overt, in which H and E are discussing H's essay.

Extract 2

H-E: I wish I could write like this

```
1   E:      um? (1.7) I ↑thought it was almost perfect.
2           (1.0)
3   H:      [hmm: .]
4   E:      [I mean] I wish=
5   H:      =[th a n k  you]
6   E:      =[I could write] (.) like this=
7   H:      =mm hm.=
8   E: →    =but uh:m (2.0) I ha::ve a question,=
9   H:      =mm hm.=
10  E: →    =about your (0.9) <first (.) reason.>
11  H: →    <mm hm.>
12          (1.3)
13  H:      yes.
14  E:      are you saying that (0.7) when you wanted your students
15          to ↑realize (.) what grammar point=
16          ((continues))
```

At the beginning of the sequence (line 1), E compliments H's essay with the somewhat emphatic and superlative term "perfect", qualified by the pitch-accented subjectivity-marker "thought" and the modifier "almost". Although this utterance is hearably completed in terms of syntax and intonation and therefore precipitates a clear possible completion point (PCP) and TRP, it is followed by a substantial silence (line 2), after which both H and E start simultaneously to vocalize (lines 3 & 4), H with an ambivalent "hmm" and E with an "I mean", projecting a reformulation, upgraded assessment, account or upshot, possibly in orientation to H's lack of response thus far. As E gets this utterance underway, H produces a clear gratitude token, "thank you", overlapping with part of E's self-deprecating praise (line 6). After another ambivalent "mm hm" from H (line 7), E clearly projects something critical to come, by prefacing with "but" and overtly indexing the action of a "question" (line 8). Although this is a hearably complete TCU and H produces a go-ahead "mm hm" (line 9) on cue in the TRP, E then syntactically extends her sentential TCU to specify the subject-matter of her question (line 10), mentioning a "first reason" (perhaps one of a series of key reasons supporting the essay's main thesis, potentially "upping the stakes" of the question to come). After another continuer there is a substantial silence (line 12), oriented to by H upgrading her "mm hm" to a "yes" (line 13), after which E launches an elaborate and evolving formulation of a Y/N polar question regarding the nature of the "reason" that H intended to write in her essay.

Reviewing the sequential structure described above, we could argue that E's first compliment could also arguably be doing the work of a pre-pre-FPP in prefacing a critical interrogative, indexed by the pre-FPP, before arriving at the base-FPP of the critical interrogative itself. Indeed, the "um?" and pause before the otherwise elegantly formulated, qualified and produced first compliment (line 1) could be the first signs of a dispreferred act to come. It may be that E's pattern of FPP utterances over the whole sequence became, paradoxically, further elaborated due to H's minimal (i.e., ambivalent) and erratically timed pre-SPPs at each stage (delay in lines 2-5; rhythmical repetition in lines 7-10; persistence/upgrading in line 13).

As we saw in this section, sequences of constructive criticism can be initiated and co-constructed with typical features of dispreferred FPPs, including delays, perturbations, mitigations, praise-as-preface, "but"-preface, and pre- and pre-pre-sequences. However, this is still assuming that a participant in this setting, who may have a warrant to offer criticism, is indeed forthcoming in initiating such an action, thus raising the following questions. Would the absence of such action be unremarkable, as a normal ("preferred") state of affairs? Or would it be "noticeably absent", as another kind of "dispreferred" state of affairs? Could a sequence with a preferred FPP be plausible in such a situation, and if so, what would it look like? The next section aims to address this.

Invitation of Criticism and its Responses

There is another type of base adjacency pair which includes criticism. In the prior sections, criticism is formulated as part of a base-FPP, but it can also occur as part of a base-SPP. When one participant takes an action that invites or requests criticism, at least some kind of criticism or advice would be expected as a preferred SPP. However, the invitation of criticism might also be declined. In this section, we introduce examples of invitations of criticism and possible responses to the invitation.

Accepting an invitation of criticism

In Extract 3, A and D are discussing D's essay. In line 1, D produces a statement of information, indexing A's ownership of a precisely quantified length of time and a projected continuity of a current state of affairs.

Extract 3
A-D: "F-rank college"

```
1   D:    you have five minutes more [hhh h]
2   A:                               [e:::?] (0.8) mmm:::
3         (2.9)
4   D: →  yeah::, (1.7) can I use in: this paragraph,((points))(1.1)
5         ah:: ef (0.4) rank (0.3) college
6         (1.3)
7   A: →  ↑yes you (0.4) can: use (0.4) ef'rank college the word,
8         [but]
9   D:    [uhn]
10  A: →  (0.7) there is (1.1) I (0.6) couldn't (0.8)
11        understand very well so [if you can]
12  D:                            [mmm. (  )]
13  A:    write more about ef'rank college (0.7)
```

A produces a stretched Japanese-style change-of-state token (line 2), followed by a pensive "mm". After a substantial silence (line 3) with no forthcoming comment, D produces an ambivalent stretched "yeah" (line 4), as if they are making a collaborative effort to find an appropriate use of the time. After another pause, he then produces a TCU-beginning which clearly projects a polar question and displays an epistemic stance of not-knowing

(K−) relative to A's possible knowing (K+) as supposed recipient of the question, thereby positioning A as potentially possessing K+ epistemic status on this matter, which is a state of affairs opposite to that of the informing in line 1. The question (lines 4-5), with an attempt to confirm mutual recognition of a relevant location in the essay, turns out to be whether he can use the word "F-rank college", which is Japanese Internet slang. In line 7, after a pause, A produces a clear affirmative "yes" to satisfy the polarity of D's question in a type-conforming positive way, then immediately begins a whole sentential TCU that recycles the question format. This turns out to be a preface to the criticism (lines 10-11), pivoting on "the word" as a qualifying appended specification and "but", which is overlapped with D's receipt (line 9) of A's affirmative answer. A's criticism, "I couldn't understand very well", is actually ambivalent, lexically softened with "very well", and hearable as either a complaint ("your term was difficult to understand") or self-deprecation ("I lacked the ability or knowledge to understand"); it is also immediately followed by a syntactically linked clause which offers a solution to the problem without having to remove or alter the expression "F-rank" itself.

Declining an invitation of criticism

Despite the criticism-inviting nature of the setting and despite an invitation to offer constructive criticism, an interactant may still decline to perform the action. Extract 4 reports an example. Prior to this sequence, T has asked Y "Are there any grammar mistakes in my essay?", and Y pointed out a very minor one. After that, Y reciprocally asks T "how about my" (line 1).

Extract 4
T-Y: grammar mistakes
```
1   Y: →  °how about my°
2   T:    hh
3   Y:    ha ha ha
4   T:    my grammar skill is very low:
5   Y:    aha ha ha  [no no no  ]
6   T: →             [so I could]n't [f i n d  any:]
7   Y:                              [I don't think] so
8         I don't think so
9   T: → I couldn't couldn't find any uh grammar mistakes in your
10        essays (.hhh)
11  Y:    thank you
```

The format of Y's question-beginning ("How about ... you/your/my ... ") is a typical one for reciprocating an enquiry, as an open-ended question with indexing of the recipient's territory of experience or knowledge. Although it is not syntactically completed, T's soft out-breath laughter-token (line 2) seems to fit Y's quiet production. Y's laughter in line 3 makes this pattern of alignment through non-serious orientation a little more overt, and seems to serve as a cue for T to begin a meaningful response (line 4) as the preface to a proper SPP to follow Y's opening FPP. T's preface is a self-deprecatory assessment of his ability in English grammar, which turns out to be an account for inability to provide constructive criticism (line 6 & lines 9-10). However, the preface is also a sentential TCU with an ambivalent PCP (syntactical only, with stretched last sound projecting possible continuation), at which point Y provides more laughter immediately leading into a preferred-shape disagreement for such a self-deprecation (Pomerantz, 1984) ("no no no I don't think so"; lines 5 & 7). The overlapping talk in this context with rival claims to turn (lines 5 & 6; 6 & 7) seems to be affiliative, but is resolved with marked retrieval with re-starts of the respective sentential TCUs (Jefferson, 1984b), though in opposite order to their first tellings. This order reversal may be linked to Y's precedence with non-overlapped laughter in line 5, but also leads to T's final unchallenged rejection of Y's invitation of criticism (lines 9-10) as a type-appropriate SPP to Y's opening FPP, with the self-deprecation-disagreement sequence tucked in between as a somewhat unorthodox insertion sequence. That T's rejection is prefaced with an account suggests a dispreferred SPP in the context.

A tentative comparison of these single cases of criticism openings presented here suggests that criticism-invitation-FPPs may be in relatively preferred formats compared with criticism-FPPs. However, criticism as an invited SPP may be treated by its speaker as equally dispreferred as criticism as a FPP, yet declining an invitation to criticize can also be dispreferred and considered to require an account.

Responses to Criticism or Advice

In the prior sections, we examined how the participants open criticism sequences. In this section, we look at how the participants respond to criticism.

Response with agreement

In Extract 5, K points out S's typographical error. In response to that, S displays his agreement with K through aligned self-criticizing, "I do this frequently" (line 9).

Extract 5
K-S: "leaning" vs. "learning"
```
1  K:    and or (hhh) the mistake e:m, (.) the letter (0.8)
2        letter of (.) >maybe,< this one, {learning (0.6) o:ther
3        (1.4)/((K pointing his finger at printed out essay))}
4  S:    ah [ha yeah: :]
5  K:       [three line]
6  S:    ha ha leaning=
7  K:    =the third li- yeah leaning (.)
8        yeah it's a [°mistake°]
9  S: →              [I do this] frequently h h a cut
```

This sequence shows a typical turn shape of agreement (i.e., performed without delay, mitigation, or accounts [Pomerantz, 1984]). However, Extract 6 shows that not all agreements are performed without delay. In Extract 6, A and D are discussing D's essay. A points out that D wrote a new idea in the conclusion though it should be written in a body paragraph. Therefore, A makes a suggestion for making one more body paragraph.

Extract 6
A-D: the conclusion
```
1  A:    but (0.5) ah::: (1.5) (.hhh) mmto:: in conclusion
2        you have one new idea
3  D:    un
4  A:    the about scholarship,
5  D:    un
6  A:    (.h) so:: (1.3) if you can write (0.6) another (0.4)
```

```
7         body: (.) n? third body paragraph,
8    D:   un
9    A:   about the scholarship? and you (1.2) can write (0.7)
10        only the conclusion in conclusion,
11   D: → ↑mmm.
12   A:   it's better I think.
13        (1.4)
14   D: → good
```

In lines 1 to 4, A gives information about what is problematic in D's essay, saying "in conclusion you have one new idea about scholarship" with continuous intonation, then proffers a suggested solution (lines 6-10). During the above, D offers minimal go-ahead/continuer-type "un" utterances (lines 3, 5 & 8), but after A's criticism and advice has been fully formulated, reacts with the markedly different "↑ mmm", a change-of-state token (Heritage, 1984), that is deployed to publicly display the participants' cognitive change from non-knowing to now-knowing, though not necessarily agreement. A ends her multi-TCU turn, saying "it's better I think", with falling intonation (line 12). After a silence, D gives a positive assessment (line 14).

D's assessment is preceded by a significant silence (line 13). This delay generally prefaces disagreement (Pomerantz, 1984). Moreover, D's plain "good" may be a weak agreement token, which is also a recurrent feature of disagreement prefaces (Pomerantz, 1984). However, it turns out that these interactional objects of D's do not lead to disagreement. Extract 7 immediately follows Extract 6. A starts a retelling with laughter (line 2), and D starts displaying his alignment to A's suggestion (line 5).

Extract 7
Following from Extract 6

```
1        (0.8)
2   A:   h h h (.hh) maybe so you can [write]
3   D:                                 [uhn  ]
4   A:   thr [ee body]
5   D: → [like a ] third[ly::]
6   A:                  [yes:] yes
7        (0.7)
8   D:   yeah
         ((lines omitted))
21  A:   [it's] (1.6) conclusion so:: (1.0) un in conclusion,=
22  D: → =LIKE' A JUSTA
23  A:   just=
24  D:   =THAT'S WHY
25  A:   >yeah yeah [yeah< h h h ]
26  D:              [I DON'T AGREE]
27  A:   yes and (0.5) if you (0.4) n? you can write (.)
28       the (0.8) points?
29  D:   uh huh
30  A:   only the points? (0.5) at the (0.9)
31  D:   ah:: yes (.) [y e s ]
32  A:                [of the] body (0.3) three body paragraphs
```

In lines 2 and 4, A starts retelling her prior suggestion (lines 6-7 of Extract 6) that D should insert a third paragraph. In the former extract, D's participation in interaction was rather passive. However, in lines 4 to 6, A and D collaboratively complete A's retelling. After that sequence, they also collaboratively make a solution (lines 21-32). D's proffered completions of A's TCUs (lines 5 & 22), raised voice, and embedded projection of his own writer's voice (line 5: "Thirdly:"; lines 24 & 26: "That's why I don't agree") arguably constitute a demonstration of his strongly aligned agreement.

With regard to preference, the turn shape of agreement as found in Extract 5 is formatted as a preferred action; it is sequence-closing relevant, and is an unmarked turn shape. On the other hand, the agreement in Extract 6 is done with an ambivalent format, somewhat dispreferred, and therefore possibly interpreted as projecting a disagreement.

Response with disagreement

In the prior section, we saw one possible response to criticism. In this section, we shall see another possible alternative response to criticism: disagreement. In Extract 8, K and S are discussing S's essay. K starts expressing a criticism of S's use of commas (lines 6-7).

Extract 8

K-S: comma

```
1   K:    em (2.9) >°a- a-°<I think that (0.9) the (3.0)
2         sixth line?
3   S:    maybe=
4   K:    =the comma- about the comma? (.hhh)
5   S:    environment=
6   K:    =the after >yeah< environment this: ((points))
7    →    should be (0.8) period? (0.8) (.h) isn't it?
8         (3.6) ((S leans forward, rubbing his nose))
```

```
9   K:    °o-° or I might be mistaken
10  S:    um
11        (2.0)
12  K:    no?
13        (0.9)
14  S: →  <yeah> it's em (1.2) ↑yeah (1.0) >yeah< period is better
15     →  maybe (.h) but then (1.1) >you know< I lived in (   )
16        three years comma (.)
17  K:    [un]
18  S:    [and] which means th't I was in (    )(0.6) environment
19  K:    un
20  S: →  this is um you know this is (.) this ah:: (1.5) inserted
21        (0.9)
22  K:    un un (1.1) ah:: okay=
23        ((continues S's account))
```

K's opening of "I think that", in his hesitant utterance in lines 1 to 2, projects a substantial assessment-centred turn involving an independent "that"-clause. The continuations of this utterance ("the ... sixth line") are syntactically positioned as the subject-phrase of this projected clause. However, "sixth line?", with its rising intonation (albeit no significant pause) is also hearable as a try-mark to seek mutual recognition of a location within S's essay, leading into further collaborative location-recognition work (lines 2-6) involving a "comma" that apparently appears after the word "environment" in S's essay. K's related self-repair work in line 4 produces a new phrasal TCU ("about the comma?"), which appears to function simultaneously as a further increment in seeking recognition of location and as a preliminary seeking a go-ahead for an assessment of the use of that comma. The collaborative recognition-seeking work culminates in K pointing at the comma on the page and using the location pro-term "this" (line 6), and this leads immediately into K's critical comment (line 7), with some pauses and a tag-question, that the comma should be a period. The pauses and rising intonation both on "period" and the tag question emphasize the tentative epistemic stance in the suggestion, the PCP, and the seeking of a response; yet although S recognizes which point K is mentioning, there is no immediate response. In orientation to the substantial silence (line 8), K appends a further epistemic downgrader ("or I might be mistaken"), formatted as a TCU syntactically contiguous to his previous turn (despite the compromised progressivity), which elicits a minimal "um" from S (line 10). After a further silence, K reformulates his previous tag question as a minimal "no?" (line 12). After another silence, from line 14, S produces a hesitant series of token agreement markers ("yeah"), an abandoned sentence-beginning ("it's em") and pauses. The last "yeah" prefaces the alignment-orienting phrase "period is better", yet this is immediately downgraded with "maybe", which in turn leads into "but then", projecting not only a disagreement but an account for a disagreement. S does the telling of his account in lines 15 to 20 with some self-repair work, culminating in the final statement, "this is inserted", implying that a comma would, after all, be the most appropriate punctuation in such a place. After a brief silence, K produces receipt tokens ("un un"), followed by a pause followed by a markedly different if ambivalent change-of-state token ("ah::") and agreement token "okay".

In this extract, K mitigates his criticism and suggestion mainly through epistemic downgraders. If S noticed an error in his comma use at that point, he could have pre-empted K's criticism with his own telling. S's progressive problematic responses to K's criticism would have been observable by K, who appears to progressively adjust his epistemic stance, almost to the point of neutralizing his own criticism (already constructed as dispreferred), thereby also potentially neutralizing the possibility of a dispreferred response (disagreement) from S. S prefaces his disagreement with hesitation and weak agreement tokens, yet nonetheless orients to disagreement with the contrastive "but". This extract thus illustrates the delicate moment-by-moment sequence adjustments in articulation with preference organization that can evolve through the accomplishment of a dispreferred FPP followed by a dispreferred SPP.

Discussion and Conclusion

In the present study, in a conversation analysis of Japanese EFL learners' criticism actions in a peer-feedback setting, we described in detail some characteristic interactional practices the participants employed in co-constructing and accomplishing sequences of constructive criticism. Participants occasionally display through their interactional practices their orientations to the setting, in which there are warrants and normative expectant pressure for constructive criticism to be proffered both ways. Nonetheless, criticism actions still tend to be prefaced by preliminaries, praise, and the contrastive conjunction "but". In addition, two types of openings for criticism sequences were observed, with two types of FPPs: a proffer of criticism and an invitation of criticism. As for the possible responses to these FPPs, it was observed that proffering criticism makes relevant agreement or disagreement as SPPs, and invitation of criticism makes relevant the on-cue proffering of criticism or the avoidance of criticism by self-deprecation.

Almost any kind of action throughout a sequence of constructive criticism seemed to have some potentially dispreferred aspect, meaning that preference organisation appears to be particularly delicate and complex in this particular setting, perhaps due to the factors discussed by Waring (2017). This made sequence-expansion relevant, even if it was invited by the author of the essay. Proffering criticism may emerge as a dispreferred FPP or as a dispreferred SPP. On the other hand, invitation of criticism itself seems rarely mitigated or delayed. Therefore, it might be tentatively suggested that invitation of criticism is preferred over proffering of criticism. With regard to SPPs following criticism FPPs, it was observed that agreement is not always done with a preferred format. Linguistic and interactional resources for constructing turn-by-turn epistemic stance, and relatedly, invoking participants' epistemic status, were displayed time and again, as were interactional practices (i.e., competences) for indexing and telling accounts, and "reading" projected completions and prospective actions in each other's turns.

Limitations of the study include the small scale of the collection and potential issues in the authenticity of the interactional setting. Future research could involve larger accumulated collections from talk-in-interaction in a wide range of non-research-purpose-settings among participants of various levels of experience in communicating in English. As for the training of EFL learners in the interactional practices described in this study, Wong and Waring (2010) may be one adaptable CA-based resource. Although its chapter on type-specific sequences does not include criticism or advice, the principles of the awareness-raising and practical activities in the book could be adapted for designing similar activities for awareness-raising and practice related to criticism and advice. In addition, Stokoe's (2011) conversation-analytic role-play method (CARM) could be used to with extracts from this study. For example, revealing one line at a time on a projector screen and having learners imagine and role-play possible next turns could be helpful for both awareness-raising and practice.

Acknowledgements

The authors would like to thank the participants who cooperated with this study and consented to having their peer-feedback sessions recorded and analysed. They are also grateful for great patience and professionalism afforded by the editors of this book.

References

Butler, C. W., Potter, J., Danby, S., Emmison, M., & Hepburn, A. (2010). Advice-implicative interrogatives: Building "client-centered" support in a children's helpline. *Social Psychology Quarterly, 74*, 216–241.

Don, Z. M., & Izadi, A. (2013). Interactionally achieving face in criticism-criticism response exchanges. *Language & Communication, 33*, 221–231.

Fujioka, M. (2013). From praise to critique in offering peer feedback on writing. In R. Chartrand, S. Crofts, & G. Brooks (Eds.), *The 2012 Pan-SIG Conference Proceedings* (pp. 86–91). Tokyo: JALT Central Office.

Goodwin, C., & Heritage, J. (1990). Conversation analysis. *Annual Review of Anthropology, 19*, 283–307.

House, J., & Kasper, G. (1981). Politeness markers in English and German. In F. Coulmas (Ed.), *Conversational routine: Explorations in standardized communication situations and prepatterned speech* (pp. 157–185). New York, U.S.A.: Mouton Publishers.

Heritage, J. (1984). A change-of-state token and aspect of its sequential placement. In J. M. Atkinson & J. Heritage (Eds.), *Structures of social action: Studies in conversation analysis* (pp. 299–345). Cambridge, U.K.: Cambridge University Press.

Heritage, J. (2012). Epistemics in action: Action formation and territories of knowledge. *Research on Language and Social Interaction, 45*(1), 1–29.

Heritage, J., & Sefi, S. (1992). Dilemmas of advice: Aspects of the delivery and reception of advice in interactions between health visitors and first-time mothers. In P. Drew & J. Heritage (Eds.), *Talk at work* (pp. 359–417). Cambridge, U.K.: Cambridge University Press.

Hutchby, I. (1995). Aspects of recipient design in expert advice-giving on call-in radio. *Discourse Process, 19*, 219–238.

Jefferson, G. (2004a). Glossary of transcript symbols with an introduction. In G. H. Lerner (Ed.), *Conversation analysis: Studies from the first generation* (pp. 13–34). Amsterdam, The Netherlands: John Benjamins.

Jefferson, G. (2004b). A sketch of some orderly aspects of overlap in natural conversation. In G. H. Lerner (Ed.), *Conversation analysis: Studies from the first generation* (pp. 43–62). Amsterdam, The Netherlands: John Benjamins.

Kinnell, A. M., & Maynard, D. (1996). The delivery and receipt of safer sex advice in pre-test counselling sessions for HIV and AIDS. *Journal of Contemporary Ethnography, 24*, 405–437.

Lerner, G. H. (1996). Finding "face" in the preference structures of talk-in-interaction. *Social Psychology Quarterly, 59*(4), 303–321.

Levinson, S. C. (1983). *Pragmatics*. Cambridge, U.K.: Cambridge University Press.

Limberg, H., & Locher, M.A. (Eds.) (2012). *Advice in discourse*. Amsterdam, The Netherlands: John Benjamins.

MEXT. (2011). *The revisions of the courses of study for elementary and secondary schools*. Retrieved from http://www.mext.go.jp/en/policy/education/elsec/title02/detail02/_icsFiles/afieldfile/2011/03/28/1303755_001.pdf

MEXT. (2014). *English education reform plan corresponding to globalization*. Retrieved from http://www.mext.go.jp/en/news/topics/detail/_icsFiles/afieldfile/2014/01/23/ 1343591_1.pdf

Mochizuki, A. (Ed.), Kubota, A., Iwasaki, H., & Ushiro, Y. (2012). *Shin gakushuu shidoo yoryoo ni motoduku eigoka kyooikuhoo* [*Teaching English as a foreign language based on the new Course of Study*]. Tokyo: Taishukan-Shoten.

Nguyen, T. T. M. (2007). *Learning to give and respond to peer-feedback in the L2: The case of EFL criticisms and responses to criticism*. Munich, Germany: LINCOM.

Nguyen, T. T. M. (2008a). Criticizing in an L2: Pragmatic strategies used by Vietnamese EFL learners. *Intercultural Pragmatics, 5*(1), 41–66.

Nguyen, T. T. M. (2008b). Modifying L2 criticisms: How learners do it? *Journal of Pragmatics, 40*, 768–791.

Nguyen, T. T. M., & Basturkmen, H. (2010). Teaching constructive critical feedback. In D. H. Tatsuki & N. R. Houck (Eds.), *Pragmatics: Teaching speech acts* (pp. 125–140). Alexandria, U.S.A.: TESOL.

Park, I. (2012). Seeking advice: epistemic asymmetry and learner autonomy in writing conferences. *Journal of Pragmatics, 44*(14), 2004–2021.

Peräkylä, A., & Silverman, D. (1991). Reinterpreting speech-exchange systems: Communication formats in aids counseling. *Sociology, 25*(4), 627–651.

Pomerantz, A. (1984). Agreeing and disagreeing with assessments: Some features of preferred/dispreferred turn shapes. In J. M. Atkinson & J. Heritage (Eds.), *Structures of social action: Studies in conversation analysis* (pp. 57–101). Cambridge, U.K.: Cambridge University Press.

Sacks, H. (1995). *Lectures on conversation, Vols. I, II*. G. Jefferson (Ed.), with introductions by E. A. Schegloff. Oxford, U.K.: Blackwell.

Sacks, H., & Schegloff, E. A. (1979). Two preferences in the organization of reference to persons in conversation and their interaction. In G. Psathas (Ed.), *Everyday language: Studies in ethnomethodology* (pp. 15–21). New York, U.S.A.: Irvington Publishers, Inc.

Sacks, H., Schegloff, E. A., & Jefferson, G. (1974). A simplest systematics for the organization of turn-taking for conversation. *Language, 50*(4), 696–735.

Schegloff, E. A. (1988). Presequences and indirection: Applying speech act theory to ordinary conversation. *Journal of Pragmatics, 12*, 55–114.

Schegloff, E. A. (1999). Discourse, pragmatics, conversation, analysis. *Discourse Studies, 1*(4), 405–435.

Schegloff, E. A. (2007). *Sequence organization in interaction: A primer in conversation analysis Vol. 1*. Cambridge, U.K.: Cambridge University Press.

Schegloff, E. A., Jefferson, G., & Sacks, H. (1977). The preference for self-correction in the organization of repair in conversation. *Language, 53*, 361–382.

Shaw, C., Potter, J., & Hepburn, A. (2015). Advice-implicative actions: Using interrogatives and assessments to deliver advice in mundane conversation. *Discourse*

Studies, 17(3), 317–342.

Silverman, D. (1997). *Discourses of counselling: HIV counselling as social interaction.* London, U.K.: Sage.

Stivers, T., & Sidnell, J. (2013). Introduction. In J. Sidnell & T. Stivers (Eds.), *The handbook of conversation analysis* (pp. 1–8). Chichester, U.K.: Wiley-Blackwell.

Stokoe, E. (2011). Simulated interaction and communication skills training: The 'conversation analytic role-play method'. In C. Antaki (Ed.), *Applied conversation analysis: Intervention and change in institutional talk* (pp. 119–139). Basingstoke, U.K.: Palgrave Macmillan.

Toplak, M., & Katz, A. (2000). On the uses of sarcastic irony. *Journal of Pragmatics, 32*, 1467–1488.

Tracy, K., & Eisenberg, E. (1990). Giving criticisms: A multiple goals case study. *Research on Language and Social Interaction, 24*, 37–70.

Turnbull, B. (2018). Is there a potential for a translanguaging approach to English education in Japan? Perspectives of tertiary learners and teachers. *JALT Journal, 40*(2), 101–134.

Vehviläinen, S. (2012). Question-prefaced advice in feedback sequences of Finnish academic supervisions. In H. Limberg & M. A. Locher (Eds.), *Advice in discourse* (pp. 31–52). Amsterdam, The Netherlands: John Benjamins.

Wajnryb, R. (1995). The perception of criticism: one trainee's experience. *EA Journal, 13*(1), 54–68.

Waring, H. Z. (2005). Peer tutoring in a graduate writing centre: Identity, expertise, and advice resisting. *Applied Linguistics, 26*(2), 141–168.

Waring, H. Z. (2007a). The multi-functionality of accounts in advice giving. *Journal of Sociolinguistics, 11*(3), 367–369.

Waring, H. Z. (2007b). Complex advice acceptance as a resource for managing asymmetries. *Text talk, 27*(1), 107–137.

Waring, H. Z. (2012). The advising sequence and its preference structures in graduate peer tutoring in an American university. In H. Limberg & M. A. Locher (Eds.), *Advice in discourse* (pp. 97–118). Amsterdam, The Netherlands: John Benjamins.

Waring, H. Z. (2017). Going general as a resource for doing advising in post-observation conferences in teacher training. *Journal of Pragmatics, 110*, 20–33.

Wierzbicka, A. (1987). *English speech act verbs: A semantic dictionary.* Marrickville,

Australia: Academic Press Australia.

Wong, J., & Waring, H. Z. (2010). *Conversation analysis and second language pedagogy: A guide for ESL/EFL teachers.* New York, U.S.A.: Routledge.

Appendix: Transcription Conventions
(Adapted from Jefferson, 2004a, pp. 24–31)

Transcription Symbol	Meaning
↑anyway / ↓anyway	Marked shifts into especially high or low pitch
over there.	Affirmative-like falling intonation at the end of an utterance
hello?	Interrogative-like rising intonation at the end of an utterance
she heard so,	Continuing intonation
UPPER-CASE LETTERS	Spoken especially loudly relative to the surrounding talk.
°word°	Spoken especially quietly relative to the surrounding talk
Underline	Some unusually marked form of stress (pitch and/or volume; longer = heavier)
>word<	Faster speech, compared to the surrounding talk
<word>	Slower speech, compared to surrounding talk
.hhh	A row of h's with a dot in front of it indicates an inbreath, without the dot an outbreath.
minutes:	Prolongation of immediately prior sound (more colons means longer stretching)
wor(h)d	Plosiveness, often associated with laughter, crying, coughing, etc.
(1.4)	Elapsed time of a pause or gap (in seconds)
(.)	A micro-pause (±0.1s), within or between utterances
well bec- because	A word cut-off (abandoned, or for a restart)
A: Did you?= B: =yes.	Latched utterances (no beat between turns, or between lines within one turn)
A: yes [I did] B: [oh yo]u uh	Overlapping speech: left brackets for the onset of overlap; right brackets for the end.
( ) or (word)	The transcriber could not hear, or was uncertain about what was said.
((comment))	Transcriber's comments/descriptions

# Part 3: The Acquisition of Pragmatics Through Interaction and Teaching

Exploring Implicit and Explicit Teaching Methods in EFL Education: A Cross-Genre Analysis of Topic Management Through Overlaps*

Lala U. Takeda

Abstract

This paper investigates topic management through overlaps in female student–student interactions in Japanese and American[1] conversations and problem-solving tasks. It focuses on idea and topic presentation to elucidate the extent to which functional differences in overlaps affect topic management between the two genres in each language. The results demonstrate that Japanese speakers used their interlocutors' backchannels as a bond, whilst American speakers clarified the similarity as a relay point. In problem-solving tasks, Japanese speakers developed their own ideas, whilst synchronizing with their interlocutors' utterances. Meanwhile, American speakers confirmed the similarity to add their ideas, while repeating a part of their interlocutors' utterances. The results were then summarized from a cross-linguistic and a cross-genre perspective to demonstrate that Japanese and American speakers adjusted the way they use overlaps by genres, whilst simultaneously using different ways to show consensus and solidarity or to signal the interlocutors' awareness of their interactional roles. Based on this, the author discusses what teaching methods should be provided for EFL interactions when considering intercultural communicative competence. This paper can help students communicate effectively with others in their first and second languages, and help teachers instruct students more effectively in cross-genre communication, as well as apply cross-linguistic perspectives to communicate effectively.

Keywords: implicit/explicit teaching, topic management, overlaps, cross-genre analysis, intercultural communicative competence

Introduction

Researchers in interlanguage pragmatics (Rose & Kasper, 2001; Kecskes & Assimakopoulos, 2017) and conversation analysis-based L2 interaction (Campbell-Larsen, 2017; Sert, 2017) have analyzed how EFL learners behave verbally and non-verbally in L2 interactions and discussed their pragmatic development. To help L2 speakers engage in pragmatically well-mannered interactions, it is considered important to clarify the differences (or similarities) in welcomed and encouraged conversational behavior between L1 interactions and L2 interactions. For example, Japanese speakers do not necessarily regard simultaneous talk as a cause of communicative conflict among speakers; Americans, however, often feel it is disrespectful, and compete to gain the floor (R. Hayashi, 1988). This situation may prevent speakers from engaging in smooth conversation with each other, unless they are aware of these differences.[2]

This indicates that Japanese speakers interacting in English with speakers from other countries must acquire and adopt a different conversational behavior from when talking with Japanese speakers in Japanese. However, this may differ from genre to genre. When Japanese speakers have a conversation in Japanese and in English, ways of interaction (including managing topics through overlaps) may be affected by the genre or by the relationship between the interlocutors.

Therefore, this paper investigates topic management through overlaps in student-student interactions in English and Japanese in two genres: conversations and problem-solving tasks by the same participants (in each case, the same pair of participants engaging in both tasks). Both genres were related to topic construction, focusing on cases in which students presented their own topics or ideas. The paper aims to elucidate the extent to which functional differences in overlaps affect topic management between the two genres[3] in each language. The two interaction genres above were selected because of the differences between them in how interlocutors construct and develop a topic or an idea: the former is a genre where, in general, one of the interlocutors presents her topic and her conversational partner listens and forms her own related topic to be shared, whilst in the latter, two interlocutors create new ideas through negotiation during their interaction.

An overlap here is defined as a form of simultaneous talk in which the first speaker's utterance is not disrupted by the second speaker's (Beattie, 1981). Beattie (1982) and Vatanen (2014) consider overlap to be equivalent to a turn-taking device, and exclude "continuers" (Schegloff, 1982, p. 81; Kushida, 2005, p. 29), such as backchannels, from their targets of analysis. The present study, however, comprehensively defines overlaps as any simultaneous utterances of words or sentences, regardless of turn-taking (Tannen, 1990; Sugawara, 1996). Given the specific nature of the genres chosen, this paper will focus on cooperative, rather than intrusive or competitive, overlaps (K. Murata, 1994; Tannen, 1996; Li, 2001; Truong, 2013). This study aims to answer the following research questions:

a. How do the closely acquainted dyads of English and Japanese female students manage their topics through overlaps while presenting their topics?
b. How does their topic management through overlaps differ according to the genre and language of their interactions?

Previous Studies of Overlaps

Researchers in conversation analysis (CA) (Sacks, Schegloff, & Jefferson, 1974; Schegloff, 2006; Sidnell, 2010; M. Hayashi, 2013) have analyzed overlap in terms of transition-relevance places (TRPs) and projectability, a feature of the unit which allows "participants to anticipate or predict where an instance of the unit will come to an end" (Tanaka, 1999, p. 27), to clarify where overlaps occur and how they should be dealt with in order to have a conversation without breakdown, based on systematic turn construction. These researchers took a stance of "context-shaped and context-renewing" (Butterfield, 2015, p. 101) and considered context only in terms of sequential or "intra-interactional context" (Schegloff, 1992, p. 195), not affected by social context (D. Maynard, 2006).

From a socio-contextual point of view, previous studies have compared interactions in American English with those in Japanese (Uchida, 2008; Fujii, 2012) to clarify the dynamics of communication in terms of the emergent meaning of an interaction (Lucy, 1993; Silverstein, 1993). Uchida (2008) mentions that Japanese speakers overlap their utterances more frequently to convey agreement, often with repetitions and supplements. American English speakers, on the other hand, use overlaps more for correction or objection, generally without repetitions or supplements. Fujii (2012) has focused on overlaps in problem-solving tasks, finding that in this context, Japanese interlocutors use more "overlapping repetition" (Fujii, 2012, p. 654), overlaps with the same or similar expressions to those used in the previous turn, than Americans do. However, none of these researchers have discussed topic management through overlaps from a cross-linguistic and cross-genre perspective.

Other studies have pointed out differences in the use of overlaps depending on the situation: the difficulty level in tasks (Bull & Aylett, 1998), comparison between two different genres (Ten Bosch, Oostdijk, & Boves, 2005), and the difference in intimacy level among interlocutors (Yuan, Liberman, & Cieri, 2007). However, they only focused on cross-genre or situational differences in the frequency and function of overlaps. The relationship between overlaps and the way to manage topics remains unexamined.

Method

The data consist of eleven pairs of recordings from each of the two genres (conversations and problem-solving tasks) within intimate female university student dyads. Conversations between eleven American pairs (between 19 and 23 years old) and eleven Japanese pairs (between 20 and 22 years old) were extracted from the "Mr. O Corpus." The corpus consists of dyad conversations between twenty-two female students (eleven pairs) in American English and twenty-six female students (thirteen pairs) in Japanese,[4] recorded under experimental conditions.[5] The recordings and their transcripts, as extracted from the corpus, were then analyzed. The data are summarized in Table 1.

Table 1
Outline of the Data

	Conversation		Task	
	Japanese 11 pairs	American 11 pairs	Japanese 11 pairs	American 11 pairs
Duration (min.:sec.)	56:31	56:51	78:40	82:01
Turn Total	1987	1053	2353	1735
Overlap Total	749	380	731	502

In the conversation genre, the participants were asked to take about five minutes to discuss something that surprised them; because of the chosen topic, this genre included some aspects of storytelling, as opposed to conversation. This paper regards storytelling as a legitimate part of the conversation genre (Jefferson, 1978; Karatsu, 2012).

In the task genre, each dyad worked together, without a time limit, to construct a coherent story using a set of fifteen picture cards from a French picture book entitled *Mister O* (Trondheim, 2003, as cited in Ide, 2014, p. 27). When conducting this task, the participants were told that there is no "correct" story. After finishing the task, participants were asked to tell their coherent story to the experimenter, one by one.

The cards in Figure 1 depict the following story: Mr. O tries to get across a ravine with the help of a bigger person, however when the bigger person picks Mr. O up, it bounces off him and lands on the other side of the ravine. Mr. O tries to do the same with a smaller person but the smaller person crushes him instead.

Figure 1 Picture Cards of Task Genre for Intimate Female Dyads. (Ide, 2014, p. 27).

Results

Conversations

A qualitative analysis was conducted to determine some of the functions of overlaps in topic management in American English and Japanese. First, in Excerpt 1, Japanese participants used their interlocutors' backchannels as a bond to continue their topic in conversation (see Appendix A for transcription conventions and Appendix B for abbreviations in the interlinear gloss):

Excerpt 1 (J-08_Cnv: Conversation_Japanese)

101   L: *nanka ne* (.) *sono ko ga kondo* (.) *shugyoo   no michi ni hairu toka*
          like   FP   its   boy SP next.time ascetic-practices LK way at enter and.such

          it{te   daigaku wo yameta no ne
          say.and   university O   quit   N FP

        'And the guy said he decided to become a Buddhist priest, or something like that, and quit the university.'

102   R: [*e::* (.) *he{::*
          oh   well

        'Oh, really? Is that so?'

103 → L: [*un* (.) *sore o kiite* (.) *suggoi bikkurishite::*=
                 yeah it O hear.and very be.surprised.and

        'Yeah. When I heard that story, I was very surprised.'

104   R: =*bikkuri   da* [*ne::*
                                 be.surprised CP FP

                         'What a surprising story that is!'

105 → L: [*un* (.) *nanka*
                                  yeah like

ne:: (..) *sooiu   kanji   no ko janai n da* [*yo*
FP   that.kind.of impression LK boy not.be N CP FP

'Right. I thought he was the last person who would talk about ascetic practices.'

106   R: [*a{::::*
                            ah

                        'Ah.'

107 → L: [*nanka ne::* (.) *pankukei*
                         like   FP   punk.descent

na no@

is FP

'He looks like a punk-rock musician.'

The interaction above developed in relation to an episode where one of L's friends quit the university to become a Buddhist priest. In this excerpt, after acknowledging R's surprised backchannel reactions in lines 102, 104, and 106, L uses these reactions as a bond and as overlaps to continue her own story in lines 103, 105, and 107. The term "bond" here is used like a *norishiro* (in paper crafting, an edge of paper left for applying glue) in Japanese. It means L's story goes smoothly even if these overlapping responses are not there.

Americans, on the other hand, clarified the similarity as a relay point to add their description, as shown in the excerpt below:

Excerpt 2 (E-20_Cnv: Conversation_English)

47   R: I was like "this is against the law in the U.S. and here I guess it's against the law to ride the bike (.) on the road."@

48   L: Yeah

49   R: But, um (.) what's surprising? I was kind of surprised by (.) how rude Japanese people can be,

50   R: I mean, not that they're more rude than American people, but,

51   L: There's like a ste[reotype

52 → **R:**   [**There's like** a stereotype that everyone's very polite, and I was like, "Whoa"

53   L: Yeah.

The topic of this excerpt is an incident related to riding bikes on the sidewalk in Japan (the participant used the word "road" to mention this). Here, L's reaction in line 51 can be regarded as a supplement to R's storytelling. R overlaps in line 52 by repeating L's previous phrase to clarify the similarity as a relay point and add her description. The author uses the term "relay point" to indicate that this overlapping part is necessary to complete R's topic. It means her story cannot be connected without the overlapping part, and that without it, the development of the story cannot be understood.

Problem-Solving Tasks

In problem-solving tasks, Japanese students developed their ideas while synchronizing with the relevant part of their interlocutors' utterances using overlaps. Excerpt 3 indicates this:

Excerpt 3 (J-20_Tsk: Problem-solving Tasks_Japanese)
277   L: *nosete   yo tte   yu*[*te*
           give.a.ride.and   FP QT   say.and
           'The small character says, "please give me a ride."'
278   R: [*un* (.) *is*[*sho   ni   watatte   yo   tte   it*[*tara* (.) *fumidai*
                                    yeah   together at cross.and FP   QT   said:if   spring.board
       ni sare (.)
       at be.made
           'And it asks the bigger character to cross the ravine together, but the small character is shaped like a springboard.'
279 → L: [*nottara* (.)
                                   get.on:if
                                   'Right after getting on.'

280 → L: [*tara* (.) *fumidai ni*
                                     if   spring.board at
     sarechat[*te*
     made.and
                            'After getting on, it is used as a springboard.'

281   R: [*te*
              and
              'And.'

282   R: *jibun ha kocchi ni oiteki*[*bori   de*
         self TP   this   at leave.behind and
         'The small character is left behind.'

283 → L: [*bori   de* (.) *po::n tte icchatte* (.) *are* (.) *okashii*
                           leave.behind and   boing QT go.and   hey be.strange
        na (.) *ja* (.) *jibun mo soo sureba   ii   n   da* (.) *to   omo*(.)*tte* (.)
        FP   then   self also that do:if be.good N CP   QT   think.and
        'Right, and the bigger character jumps boing. But the small character soon notices
        like, "Hey, what happened? It seems strange." Then, the small character decides that it should
        imitate what the bigger character did.'

In this excerpt, line 279 is a paraphrase, used as an attempt to continue from line 277. However, this paraphrase does not contribute to L's topic development because of R's continuous talk in line 278. L restarts in line 280, using "*tara*" as her paraphrase of R's utterance "*ittara fumidai ni sare*" in line 278, though this is also unsuccessful. Then, L's utterances in lines 279 and 280 cannot be used as clues to develop her own idea.

On the other hand, after synchronizing in line 283 with "*bori de*," L finally finds a chance to develop her idea for describing the cards. This synchronization is an example of "overlapping repetition" (Fujii, 2012, p. 654), which occurs "when one speaker constructs an utterance based on the immediately co-present utterance of a dialogic partner" (Du Bois, 2014, p. 360). Expressions in "overlapping repetition" (Fujii, 2012, p. 654) encourage each other to activate and elaborate certain aspects of the perceived relationship between paired linguistic elements based on their similarities (cf. Du Bois, 2014, p. 372). This activation makes L ensure that her idea of how to describe the cards is the same as that of her interlocutor. This encourages her to develop the current idea with an effect of resonance, defined by Du Bois (2014, p. 360) as "the catalytic activation of affinities across utterances."

The next excerpt demonstrates that American participants confirmed similarity to add their own ideas, while repeating a part of their interlocutors' utterances:

Excerpt 4 (E-22_Tsk: Problem-solving Tasks_English)

69　　L: Hmm, yeah, [and he goes (.) he jumps, maybe?
70　　R:　　　　　[And (.)
71　　R: Gets on his [head, jumps,
72　→ L:　　　　　　　[**Head (..) jumps (.)** but he misses and he squishes him, and then,
73　　R: He flattens him, [he looks, here's his friend, you can tell because there's
　　　　　a little grey spot, so may[be,
74　　L:　　　　　　　　[Hmm.
75　　L:　　　　　　　　　　　　[Oh, that's his[(.)
76　→ R:　　　　　　　　　　　　　　　　　[**That's** his little outer skin or something.

L's utterance in line 72 is a supplement to line 71, which is R's answer to L's utterance in line 69, with an "overlapping repetition" (Fujii, 2012, p. 654).

This utterance can be explained as "speaking in unison" (Sugawara, 2012, p. 577) for "completing the sentences of the other" (ibid.) through overlaps.

Another focused utterance in line 76 is an overlap using a part of L's utterance in line 75 to complete the description. The utterance in line 75 is for adding a piece of information to the content in line 73, used by R as a further description of her idea of a card description. The overlap in line 76 is not regarded as an exact "overlapping repetition" (Fujii, 2012, p. 654), but a delayed repetition. Still, this overlap also includes a function of confirming the similarity, so that R can start adding her own ideas by taking advantage of the similarity in phrases and using repetition to show the commonality between the interlocutors.

Discussion

Considering the results from a cross-linguistic point of view, the author identifies two significant attitudes, also pointed out by Kosaki and Takeda (2017). In Japanese, by bonding and synchronizing, clear role boundaries are eliminated. Interlocutors exhibit consensus and solidarity to appreciate the commonality of their topic or ideas during the interaction. This is referred to as a "we-work-as-one" (Kosaki & Takeda, 2017) kind of attitude. In American English, a relay point and an addition of one's own idea after confirming similarity can be interpreted as a way of signaling that the interlocutors are aware of their individual roles in the interaction, referred to a "now-you-talk-so-I-listen" (Kosaki & Takeda, 2017) kind of attitude.

When reviewed from a cross-genre perspective, the results suggest that collaboration emerges from topic management by overlaps through situational adjustment in the interaction process. This is based on the principle that behavior may be "mainly influenced by situational factors aimed at adjusting the requirement of situations" (Wang & Cui, 2006, p. 552). It appears that such collaboration in conversation encourages rapport between participants, avoiding interaction breakdown. Overlaps in conversation, entitled atmosphere-valued interaction, place a high value on atmosphere and allow conversation to develop rhythmically, as the interlocutors frequently overlap with backchannels. In the task entitled "content-valued interaction"[6] (ibid.) on the other hand, collaboration serves to complete the story-building task by providing each participant's perspectives on the story; overlaps help build consensus on the task. According to this gradient difference[7] between atmosphere-valued and content-valued interaction, participants adjust the way they use overlaps by genre to create collaboration throughout topic management, both in American English and in Japanese.

These findings enable the author to indicate the kinds of teaching methods that should be provided for EFL interactions from the perspective of teaching interaction and intercultural communicative competence. In fact, there is a need to implicitly and explicitly introduce into conversation instruction some pragmatic rules tailored to a given genre and intimacy level for better intercultural communication (developed from Kosaki & Takeda, 2017). They suggest two-step instruction concerning implicitness and explicitness. To enhance their students' intercultural awareness, teachers should start with implicit instruction (Ishihara & Cohen, 2010; McConachy & Hata, 2013). Ishihara and Cohen (2010) describe both explicit and implicit instruction, and regard implicit instruction as an awareness-raising approach. McConachy and Hata (2013) emphasize the importance of teachers' questioning as a scaffold to facilitate learners' self-reflection.

This study's results have implications for the nurturing of intercultural communication skills in teaching English. Y. Murata (2015, p. 279) points out the existence of language-specific "pragmatic rules," that is, "the rules on how to use language" (ibid.). She argues that it is important that the teaching of English to Japanese learners should be based on Japanese pragmatic rules. She adds that explicit education should be provided on the difference between rules in Japanese and American English, because pragmatic rules greatly affect cross-cultural/cross-language communication.

On this point, Y. Murata (2015, p. 287) notes that turn-taking is governed by metalinguistic rules. Thus, it may be effective to give implicit instruction to learners about how to deal with overlaps in interactions. Murata does not distinguish between overlaps by situation when discussing pragmatic rules in a particular language; however, the results of the current study suggest that it would not be sufficient for instructors to implicitly teach a simple pragmatic rule, given the joint construction of conversation by interlocutors in genre-specific ways. This implies instead that it is necessary to more explicitly teach different pragmatic rules depending on genre to decrease difficulties in communication arising from the unsuitable transferring of pragmatic rules from one genre to another.

Based on their arguments, Kosaki and Takeda (2017) divide implicit instruction into the following four steps: (1) doing the same task (topic-based/task-based) in their L1 and L2 with teachers checking if students' L1 pragmatic norms might be transferred to interactions in their L2 while students engage in the task; (2) freely discussing some difficulties or problems students might have encountered in their interactions; (3) reflecting on students' use of overlaps with scaffolding questions[8] from teachers to promote students' discussions; and (4) identifying overlaps while listening to conversations between native speakers and discussing the similarities or differences in topic management through overlaps between the two languages. This last step welcomes anything that students notice when they examine the scripted data or listen to actual interactions, which makes it similar to a data session in CA. Moreover, students are encouraged to discuss the similarities or differences in the functions of overlaps between the two languages, which can enhance their intercultural awareness.

Furthermore, after these implicit instructions, teachers should move to explicit instruction such as role-play practice, to acquire and apply some suitable strategies in interactions between Japanese and American students. Instructors set two roles here: (1) overlapping their interlocutors' utterances to continue their own topic or idea, and (2) being overlapped by their interlocutors without attempting to re-establish dominance in the interaction.

However, teachers should be careful not to oversimplify the suggested role-play patterns or conversations they show to their students. Rather, they should share a strong awareness that the explicit instructions must be a resource for actual interactions and showcase the diversity of contexts English is used in the real world. It is a necessary and important method to acknowledge that English itself is diversified, and each student will encounter various kinds of interactions between people around the world.

From the above point of view, teachers should take this diversity, such as English as a lingua franca, into account even if they teach one model as a sample dialogue based on native speakers' perspectives. This is especially the case in light of the recent prominence given to diverse uses of English, such as "Global Englishes," "English as a Lingua Franca," and "World Englishes." These predominantly involve non-native speakers and are associated with the acceleration of globalization in Japan (K. Murata, 2016). Japanese learners of English do not always need to conform to L1 English speakers' norms; they should also be able to maintain and negotiate their own identity while using English. It is important, however, that they be aware of how this might be perceived and interpreted, even misunderstood, by others.

Conclusion

This study conducted a cross-linguistic and cross-genre analysis of overlaps to clarify that Japanese and American speakers have different genre-specific ways of approaching topic management to accomplish similar interactional purposes. Based on this difference and similarity, the author developed the idea of implicitly and explicitly teaching conversation in English from a proposal by Kosaki and Takeda (2017). They suggest the importance of pragmatically instructing interactions, both implicitly and explicitly, from a cross-linguistic point of view. This paper adds a cross-genre perspective to their study to contribute to helping students communicate effectively with others in their first and second languages and to helping teachers instruct students more effectively in communication from cross-genre and cross-linguistic perspectives.

Concurrently, however, since this study mainly focused on topic management with collaborative overlaps, further analysis is required. It should examine intrusive overlaps, how speakers deal with this type of overlap, and its contribution to developing and managing one specific topic. Moreover, the collection of data in L2 and an examination of the interlocutors' L1 transfer in their L2 should be encouraged; this would suggest implications for instruction in intercultural competence (Kosaki & Takeda, 2017). Furthermore, the development of teaching materials on topic management through overlaps would be valuable to enable teachers to present these materials to their students and instruct them in actual language classes on how to manage turn-taking and develop topics. Previous studies concerning teaching pragmatic rules (Ishihara & Cohen, 2010; McConachy & Hata, 2013; Y. Murata, 2015) can provide inspiration regarding how to develop awareness of interactional behaviors implicitly and explicitly. The introduction of both implicit and explicit instruction based on Kosaki and Takeda (2017) can have a positive effect on language learners, especially at intermediate or advanced level. However, students at a basic level also need to acquire the skill of managing topics during an interaction. Investigating weak points in beginners' knowledge can reveal how they manage turn-taking, which includes overlaps. Then, teaching methods can be arranged to accommodate students at this level — for example, incorporating chat-based relay writing into turn exchanges within interactions as training for promptly finding and using appropriate vocabulary.

Acknowledgements

This work was supported by a Grant-in-Aid for Scientific Research from the Japan Society for the Promotion of Science (No. 15K02763 [A cross-genre study of overlaps and collaboration in American and Japanese] and No. 18K00886 [A proposal of a speaking/writing integrated instruction method to teach English conversation to Japanese EFL learners]). I would like to thank Professor Sachiko Ide and Professor Yoko Fujii for their kind permission of using the "Mister O Corpus." My appreciation also goes to Megumi Okugiri for her warm support and helpful discussions.

References

Bakhtin, M. (1986). *Speech genres and other late essays*. (V. McGee, Trans.). Austin, TX: University of Texas Press.

Beattie, G. (1981). Interruptions in conversational interaction, and its relation to the sex and status of the interactants. *Linguistics, 19*, 15–35. doi: 10.1515/ling.1981.19.1-2.15

Beattie, G. (1982). Turn-taking and interruption in political interviews: Margaret Thatcher and Jim Callaghan compared and contrasted. *Semiotica, 39* (1/2), 93–114. doi: 10.1515/semi.1982.39.1-2.93

Brown, G., & Yule, G. (1983). *Discourse analysis*. Cambridge: Cambridge University Press.

Bull, M., & Aylett, M. (1998). An analysis of the timing of turn-taking in a corpus of goal-oriented dialogue. In *ICSLP 1998: The 5th International Conference on Spoken Language Processing*, 1175–1178.

Butterfield, J. (2015). Conversation analysis and the debate on social and sequential context. *Kanagawa University Studies in Humanities, 186*, 97–109.

Campbell-Larsen, J. (2017). *Emergent interactional competence: Free conversation in the classroom*. Paper presented at the CAN-ASIA Symposium on L2 Interaction (in Tokyo, Japan on May 28th). Retrieved from https://docs.wixstatic.com/ugd/b3a552_69f4989cb83a4cd2af5fe35a73daadb9.pdf

Du Bois, J. (2014). Towards a dialogic syntax. *Cognitive Linguistics, 25*(3), 359–410. doi: 10.1515/cog-2014-0024

Du Bois, J., Schuetze-Coburn, S., Cumming, S., & Paolino, D. (1993). Outline of discourse transcription. In J. Edwards & M. Lampert (Eds.), *Talking data: Transcription and coding methods for discourse research* (pp. 45–89). Hillsdale, NJ: Lawrence Erlbaum Associates.

Enomoto, T. (2014). Kooi no naka no "eikaiwa": Kan-disukoosusei ga orinasu kyooshitsu no tajuuteki jikuukan [Eikaiwa in performance: Interdiscursivity and the multiplicity of chronotopes in classrooms.] *Intercultural Communication Review, 12*, 85–102. doi: 10.14992/00011113

Fujii, Y. (2012). Differences of situating self in the place/ba of interaction between the Japanese and American English speakers. *Journal of Pragmatics, 44*(5), 636–662.

doi: 10.1016/j.pragma.2011.09.007

Hall, E. (1976). *Beyond culture*. New York: Anchor Books.

Hayashi, M. (2003). *Joint utterance construction in Japanese conversation*. Amsterdam: John Benjamins.

Hayashi, M. (2013). Turn allocation and turn sharing. In T. Stivers & J. Sidnell (Eds.), *The handbook of conversation analysis* (pp. 167–190). Malden: Wiley-Blackwell. doi: 10.1002/9781118325001.ch9

Hayashi, R. (1988). Simultaneous talk – from the perspective of floor management of English and Japanese speakers. *World Englishes, 7*(3), 269–288. doi: 10.1111/j.1467-971X.1988.tb00237.x

Ide, S. (2014). Kaihooteki goyooron to Mr. O corpus no igi: Bunka, intaa-akushon, gengo no kaimei no tame ni [Emancipatory pragmatics and significance of Mr. O corpus: For the breakthrough of culture, interaction, and language]. In S. Ide & Y. Fujii (Eds.), *Kaihooteki goyooron he no choosen: Bunka, intaa-akushon, gengo [Towards emancipatory pragmatics: Culture, interaction and language]* (pp. 1–31). Tokyo: Kuroshio.

Ishihara, N., & Cohen, A. (2010). *Teaching and learning pragmatics: Where language and culture meet*. London: Routledge.

Jefferson, G. (1978). Sequential aspects of storytelling in conversation. In J. Schenkein (Ed.), *Studies in the organization of conversational interaction* (pp. 219–248). New York: Academic Press. doi: 10.1016/B978-0-12-623550-0.50016-1

Karatsu, M. (2012). *Conversational storytelling among Japanese women*. Amsterdam: John Benjamins.

Kecskes, I., & Assimakopoulos, S. (Eds.). (2017). *Current issues in intercultural pragmatics*. Amsterdam: John Benjamins.

Kosaki, J., & Takeda, L. (2017). *Pragmatic rules as an enhancement of students' intercultural competence: A study based on a functional analysis of overlaps in problem-solving tasks*. Paper presented at the 15th International Pragmatics Conference (in Belfast, Northern Ireland on July 18th). Retrieved from https://cdn.ymaws.com/pragmatics.international/resource/collection/C57D1855-A3BB-40D8-A977-4732784F7B21/15th%20IPC%20abstracts-Belfast.pdf#search=%27Belfast%2C+Northern+Ireland%2C+1621+July+2017+abstract%27

Kushida, S. (2005). *Kaiwa ni okeru sanka no soshikika no kenkyuu: Nihongo kaiwa ni okeru "hanashite" to "kyo-seiinsei" no sanshutsu tetsuduki [A study of how participation in conversations is organized?: The procedure of producing "speaker" and "co-membership" in Japanese conversation] (Unpublished doctoral dissertation). Graduate School of Human and Environmental Studies, Kyoto University, Kyoto.

Kushida, S., Sadanobu, T., & Den, Y. (Eds.). (2005). *Shiriizu bun to hatsuwa dai ikkan katsudoo to shite no bun to hatsuwa* [Sentence and utterance, Vol. 1: Sentence and utterance as activity]. Tokyo: Hitsuji.

Li, H.Z. (2001). Cooperative and intrusive interruptions in inter- and intracultural dyadic discourse. *Journal of Language and Social Psychology, 20*(3), 259–284. doi: 10.1177/0261927X01020003001

Lucy, J. (1993). Reflexive language and the human disciplines. In J. Lucy (Ed.), *Reflexive language: Reported speech and metapragmatics* (pp. 9–32). Cambridge: Cambridge University Press. doi: 10.1017/CBO9780511621031.003

Malinowski, B. (1989[1923]). The problem of meaning in primitive languages. In C. Ogden & I. Richards (Eds.), *The meaning of meaning, supplement 1* (pp. 296–336). New York: Harcourt Brace Jovanovich.

Martin, J., & Rose, D. (2003). *Working with discourse: Meaning beyond the clause*. London: Continuum.

Maynard, D. (2006). Ethnography and conversation analysis: What is the context of an utterance? In S. Hesse-Biber & P. Leavy (Eds.), *Emergent methods in social research* (pp. 55–94). London: Sage. doi: 10.4135/9781412984034.n4

Maynard, S. (2008). *Maruchi-janruron: Kan-janrusei to imi no souzoo* [An exploration into multi-genre discourse: Inter-genre significance and the creation of meaning]. Tokyo: Kuroshio.

McConachy, T., & Hata, K. (2013). Addressing textbook representations of pragmatics and culture. *ELT Journal, 67*(3), 294–301. doi: 10.1093/elt/cct017

Murata, K. (1994). Intrusive or co-operative? A cross-cultural study of interruption. *Journal of Pragmatics, 21*(4), 385–400. doi: 10.1016/0378-2166(94)90011-6

Murata, K. (2016). Introduction: Researching ELF in academic and business contexts. In K. Murata (Ed.), *Exploring ELF in Japanese academic and business contexts: Conceptualisation, research and pedagogic implications* (pp. 1–13). London: Routledge.

Murata, Y. (2015). Goyoo-shihyoo to sono eigo kyooiku he no ooyoo [Pragmatic features and their application to English education]. In S. Tsuda, Y. Murata, M. Otani, Y. Iwata, Y. Shigemitsu, & Y. Otsuka, *Nichi-eigo danwa sutairu no taishoo kenkyuu: Eigo komyunikeeshon he no ouyoo* [*Comparative study of Japanese and English discourse styles: Application to English education of communication*] (pp. 277–291). Tokyo: Hitsuji.

Rose, D. (2012). Genre in the Sydney school. In J. Gee & M. Handford (Eds.), *The Routledge handbook of discourse analysis* (pp. 209–225). London: Routledge.

Rose, K., & Kasper, G. (Eds.) (2001). *Pragmatics in language teaching*. Cambridge: Cambridge University Press.

Sacks, H., Schegloff, E., & Jefferson, G. (1974). A simplest systematics for the organization of turn-taking for conversation. *Language, 50*(4), 696–735. doi: 10.2307/412243

Schegloff, E. (1982). Discourse as an interactional achievement: some uses of "uh huh" and other things that come between sentences. In D. Tannen (Ed.), *Analyzing discourse: Text and talk* (pp. 71–93). Washington: Georgetown University Press.

Schegloff, E. (1992). Repair after next turn: The last structurally provided defense of intersubjectivity in conversation. *American Journal of Sociology, 97*(5), 1295–1345. doi: 10.1086/229903

Schegloff, E. (2006). Accounts of conduct in interaction: Interruption, overlap and turn-taking. In J. Turner (Ed.), *Handbook of sociological theory* (pp. 287–322). New York: Plenum. doi: 10.1007/0-387-36274-6_15

Sert, O. (2017). *The interplay between collaborative sequences and active listenership: Implications for L2 IC*. Paper presented at the 15th International Pragmatics Conference (in Belfast, Northern Ireland on July 20th). Retrieved from https://cdn.ymaws.com/pragmatics.international/resource/collection/C57D1855-A3BB-40D8-A977-4732784F7B21/15th%20IPC%20abstracts-Belfast.pdf#search=%27Belfast%2C+Northern+Ireland%2C+1621+July+2017+abstract%27

Sidnell, J. (2010). *Conversation analysis: An introduction*. Oxford: Wiley-Blackwell.

Silverstein, M. (1993). Metapragmatic discourse and metapragmatic function. In J. Lucy (Ed.), *Reflexive language: Reported speech and metapragmatics* (pp. 33–58). Cambridge: Cambridge University Press. doi: 10.1017/CBO9780511621031.004

Sugawara, K. (1996). Hitotsu no koe de kataru koto: Shintai to kotoba no "doojisei" wo megutte [To speak in one voice: A discussion of "sameness" in body and language]. In K. Sugawara & M. Nomura (Eds.), *Komyunikeeshon to shite no shintai* [*The body as communication*] (pp. 246-287). Tokyo: Taishukan.

Sugawara, K. (2012). Interactive significance of simultaneous discourse or overlap in everyday conversations among |Gui former foragers. *Journal of Pragmatics*, *44*(5), 577-618. doi: 10.1016/j.pragma.2011.07.015

Swales, J. (1990). *Genre analysis: English in academic and research settings*. Cambridge: Cambridge University Press.

Tanaka, H. (1999). *Turn-taking in Japanese conversation*. Amsterdam: John Benjamins.

Tannen, D. (1990). *You just don't understand*. New York: William Morrow.

Tannen, D. (1996). *Gender and discourse*. Oxford: Oxford University Press.

Ten Bosch, L., Oostdijk, N., & Boves, L. (2005). On temporal aspects of turn taking in conversational dialogues. *Speech Communication*, *47*(1-2), 80-86. doi: 10.1016/j.specom.2005.05.009

Trondheim, L. (2003). *Mister O*. Tokyo: Kodansha.

Truong, K. (2013). Classification of cooperative and competitive overlaps in speech using cues from the context, overlapper, and overlappee. In *Proceedings of the 14th Annual Conference of the International Speech Communication Association, Interspeech 2013*, 1404-1408.

Uchida, L. (2008). Metacommunicative approach to overlaps in English and Japanese: Their purpose and distribution. *Bulletin of Tokyo Denki University, Arts and Sciences*, *6*, 63-70.

Vatanen, A. (2014). *Responding in overlap: Agency, epistemicity and social action in conversation* (Unpublished doctoral dissertation). Department of Finnish, Finno-Ugrian and Scandinavian Studies, University of Helsinki, Helsinki, Finland.

Wang, D., & Cui, H. (2006). Relations with personality and cross-situational consistency of behavior. *Acta Psychologica Sinica*, *38*, 543-552.

Wang, Y.-F., & Tsai, P.-H. (2007). Textual and contextual contrast connection: A study of Chinese contrastive markers across different text types. *Journal of Pragmatics*, *39*(10), 1775-1815. doi: 10.1016/j.pragma.2007.05.011

Yuan, J., Liberman, M., & Cieri, C. (2007). Towards an integrated understanding of speech overlaps in conversation. *Proceedings of the International Congress of*

Notes

* This paper was originally presented as "A cross-genre analysis of topic management through overlaps in student–student interactions: Its application to English language education" at a symposium during the 56th JACET International Convention, Aoyama Gakuin University, Tokyo, 31 August 2017, entitled "Contribution to English language teaching from a pragmatic approach: A discussion on English as a foreign language (EFL) textbook materials and teaching methods for conversation and writing."

[1] Following the definitions used by Fujii (2012, p. 637), who conducted a cross-linguistic and cross-cultural study using the same corpus data as this paper, throughout the article I use the term "American" as denoting US residents and "American English" as denoting English as spoken and used in the US.

[2] Concerning this kind of difference, it may also be possible to refer to the concepts of high- and low-context cultures by Hall (1976) on why there is a difference in feedback tendencies between Japanese and American speakers. In a high-context culture, such as Japan's, interlocutors rely heavily on phatic utterances, including backchannels and feedback, because they already share considerable experience and content. In a low-context culture such as America's, on the other hand, less background knowledge or contextual information is shared before the interaction begins. Thus, Americans tend to depend more on the utterance content on site.

[3] This paper defines genre as a type of interaction determined by the interrelation of the content of utterances, style of linguistic expression, and configuration structure (Bakhtin, 1986; S. Maynard, 2008; Enomoto, 2014), performed in pursuit of socially and culturally distinctive purposes (Swales, 1990; Martin & Rose, 2003; Rose, 2012).

[4] Among these, two of the Japanese pairs were excluded, for the following reasons: one had a low level of intimacy (meeting for the first time) and the other was recorded with no instruction as to time restriction in conducting the conversations.

[5] This is a cross-linguistic video corpus collected for four projects under Grants-in-Aid for Scientific Research from the Japan Society for the Promotion of Science: "Theoretical and practical investigation of the relationship among culture, language,

and interaction in Asia," "The development of an emancipatory approach concerning the relationship among culture, interaction, and language," "Towards emancipatory pragmatics: Discourse analyses from native speaker's perspectives," and "Co-creation of socio-cultural ba/field and language use: Construction of a pragmatic theory from native speakers' point of view" (Nos. 15320054 and 18320069, directed by Sachiko Ide, and 20320064 and 23320090, directed by Yoko Fujii). All the processes and interactions were DVD-recorded.

[6] These two types of interactions (atmosphere-valued and content-valued) might remind some readers of the two functions of language proposed by Brown and Yule (1983, p. 1): "interactional" and "transactional." Atmosphere-valued interaction, however, also includes an aspect of creating rhythms to develop interactions as we can imagine from the term "phatic communion" (Malinowski, 1989[1923], p. 315). Content-valued interaction is close to the "transactional" function (Brown & Yule, 1983, p. 1) in respect of "the communication of information" (Brown & Yule, 1983, p. 2); however, overlaps in content-valued interaction might not always convey "factual or propositional information" (ibid.), but rather might often express opinions and "the feelings of the speaker" (Wang & Tsai, 2007, p. 1805), such as agreement and empathy.

[7] The gradience in these two kinds of interactions means that there might be more ways of interacting than simply "for atmosphere" or "for content." For example, engaging in and perpetuating the conversation is also a task, and some conversations are much more goal-oriented than others. Conversely, some tasks are very loose, such as some games or free play. Or, in work contexts, for example, two possible points of discussion arise: (1) how conversation that is ostensibly task-unrelated contributes to achievement of work goals; and (2) how overlaps can be used in a different way to achieve goals in hierarchicalized settings.

[8] Kosaki and Takeda (2017) provide examples of scaffolding questions, such as "Were you aware of managing topics by using overlaps during the interaction?" and "Did you feel comfortable or uncomfortable with your partner's overlapped talk, and why?"

Appendix A: Transcription conventions

(Adapted from Du Bois, Schuetze-Coburn, Cumming, & Paolino, 1993; Kushida, Sadanobu, & Den, 2005)

[XX: beginning of overlaps =: latching (no gap after the previous utterance)
'XX': English translation of Japanese conversation
→ : places where overlaps occur (..): pause, more than a half second
(.): micro-pause @: laughter
.: falling intonation ,: continuing intonation
:: lengthened syllable ?: rising intonation

Appendix B: Abbreviations in the interlinear gloss

(Adapted from M. Hayashi, 2003, pp. 241-242)

CP various forms of copula verb *be*   FP final particle
LK nominal linking particle   N nominalizer
O object particle   QT quotative particle
SP subject particle   TP topic particle

From Needs Analysis to Emergent Pragmatic Competence: A Longitudinal Micro-Analytic Study of Learner Talk in Japanese EFL University Classes

John Campbell-Larsen

Abstract

English is a compulsory subject in the Japanese education system. However, it is widely recognized that Japanese learners of English often have difficulties engaging in spontaneous spoken interactions in English, even after several years of formal study (Dwyer & Heller-Murphy, 1996; Ellis, 1991; Pritchard & Maki, 2006). These difficulties often seem to be centered on pragmatic and interactional issues. Even learners with high scores on formal English language tests may find it difficult to engage in spontaneous spoken interaction. Further teaching and testing of grammar and vocabulary is unlikely to develop the pragmatic and interactional skills of learners. This paper outlines a project to identify and address certain pragmatic aspects of students' speaking. A focus on such areas as sequencing, repair and use of discourse markers, alongside regular opportunities to engage in unscripted non-goal-directed conversation led to developments in the learners' interactional competence.

Keywords: conversation, language learning, interactional competence

The Data

The data in this study is derived from video-recorded classroom interactions between learners of English as a foreign language at a university in Japan. The subjects were Japanese native speakers in their early twenties, roughly balanced between male and female. The class met twice a week for 90 minutes each session over two 15-week semesters. The teacher recorded the data on a hand-held video camera. Conversation partners were self-selected by the participants, as was topic. No task, goal or time limit was specified other than for the participants to conduct a conversation using English as much as possible. The teacher moved from group to group and recorded approximately five minutes of ongoing conversation. Most conversations were dyadic but some involved three participants. While the recording was in progress the other class members were also conducting their conversations freely elsewhere in the classroom. Recordings were made three times during the academic year, in April, July and January, labeled *Pre*, *Post* and *Final* respectively. The group members were not always the same, although some pairs did remain fixed across the three recordings. The data was collected over three years, labeled as *AEI*, *AEII* and *AEIII*. giving approximately 300 minutes of data. After the recordings were made the files were transcribed according to Jeffersonian transcription conventions (see Psathas & Anderson, 1990 and appendix).

Data Overview: *Pre*

The videos recorded in April of each year (*Pre*) were made early in the course, when many of the students had only brief acquaintance with each other (although some students did have more extensive prior acquaintance).

The amount of speaking that took place varied considerably. A rough count of words in a 'cleaned up' version of the transcripts shows that the total number of hearable words uttered in the interactions ranged from approximately 150 to approximately 340 over the five-minute duration of the recording. There were stark individual differences in the amount of speaking, with some speakers producing a number of lengthy turns and others producing a much more limited number of short turns. All interactions featured a mixture of both English and Japanese utterances, from code switching to supply an unknown word whilst maintaining an overall orientation to continuing the interaction in English, to abandonment (or at least suspension) of the English interaction to engage in a multi-turn sequence in Japanese. Use of L1 was observed in all of the *Pre* conversations by all participants, but the frequency and function of these L1 utterances was highly individuated.

Another commonality of the *Pre* conversations was the prevalence of very short turns, consisting of a single, sentence level proposition (or at least an attempt to produce one) or a single, unelaborated question. Grammar infelicities and pausing were also common. Some speakers engaged in repeated pauses while others proceeded more or less smoothly through most of their turns, even if grammatical or lexical infelicities were present.

Detailed analysis of the *Pre* transcripts revealed an almost complete absence of common English discourse markers (DM). Words and expressions such as *well, you know, I mean* and so on were not a regular feature of any of the conversations. Even the more fluent students utilized these words sparsely or not at all. The high frequency of common DM is noted by McCarthy (2010). Their almost complete absence from student talk is noteworthy.

Although common DM were almost completely absent from the conversations, the marker *so* was very prominent. This word, as with other English discourse markers, has a variety of meanings and functions. The talk of several speakers was replete with multiple occurrences of this word, as in the following excerpt.

Excerpt 1

AEIII Pre 108

```
01. A: So <then I was> sleeping so suddenly my smart
02.     phone ah so alarm I have never heard sound so
03.     what's this so I surprised and watched so I have
04.     never seen message so what what so I thought so
05.     (.)so (.) I thought so so happened a earthquake
06.     so I (1.0) so only I saw si. sit I can't do so
07.     stop earthquake uh:::so stopped it and I put on
08.     Tee vee pee see and smart phone and opened door
09.     so I couldn't sleep earthquake happened I'm
10.     getting information about earthquake so about two
11.     hours so my family sleep again so two hours I I
12.     didn't sleep I at eight am so I went out to come
13.     this university
```

There are multiple occurrences of the word *so* this excerpt, often seemingly deployed to hold the turn while processing the next utterance. This over-reliance on *so* may be connected to the existence of the near homonym *sou* in Japanese, which, like English *so*, is extremely polysemous.

Backchannel

In spoken interaction, while one person is speaking, the other interactant(s) do not sit silently listening to the current speaker's talk. Rather, current non-turn holders show that they are actively involved in the interaction by various linguistic and non-linguistic means such as nodding, smiling, using lexical (*yeah, right, no*) and non-lexical (*uh huh, hmmm*) utterances to show engagement, understanding, agreement and so on. Such behaviors are referred to variously as *backchanneling* (Yngve, 1970) or *reactive tokens* (Clancy, Thompson, Suzuki, & Tao, 1996). In Japanese these are termed *Aizuchi* (see LoCastro, 1987). They include words such as *hai, sou* and non-lexical utterances such as *ehh, uhn* and are often prolonged with distinct intonational contours.

In the *Pre* recordings, use of Japanese style *aizuchi* was widespread, although with individual differences. Excerpt 2 illustrates the phenomenon.

Excerpt 2
AE1 Pre 0002
```
01. Mayu:  I have Teki (0.2) dakara I want to (.) etoh
02.        Sanomiya [or >Umeda<]
03. Kana:           [U::::::::h] A:::::hhhh=
04. Mayu:  =want to(.) [new job  ]
05. Kana:              [ A::::::::]::::::::::h(.) Sanomiya
```

In this excerpt speaker Mayu is explaining places she wants to visit in the Kansai urban area. In line 03 Kana responds with prolonged *aizuchi*. In line 03 the first utterance is in overlap with Mayu and is immediately followed by another extended utterance in the clear. In line 05, Kana's *aizuchi* starts off in overlap and continues well past the end of Mayu's utterance (see Clancy, Thompson, Suzuki, & Tao, 1996 on the placement and frequency of *aizuchi* in Japanese). In effect, we can say that although Kana is speaking in English, she is listening in Japanese.

L1 Utterances

As was mentioned above, all of the *Pre* conversations featured use of the L1. One extremely common occurrence was the use of L1 discourse markers such as *etoh, anno* and so on. These words roughly correspond to words like *well, you know,* and *I mean,* in English. The occurrence was observed in excerpt 2, line 01 above. Following are further illustrative excerpts.

Excerpt 3
AEI Pre 0002
```
01. Kana:   form (.) former?
02. Mayu:   >etoh< home my my >etoh< I I was bornu in Kobe
03.         butuh etoh:: eto:h ssss. Sugu go to Shizuoka
```

Excerpt 4
AEII Pre 0068
```
01. A:   I worked (.) call center izu very (.) busy.
02.      (2.3)
03. K:   I also etoh (.) work (.) worked eh:: Sun.
04.      Saturday.
```

Use of L1 DM was widespread, but highly individuated, with some interactants saturating their talk with Japanese DMs and others uttering them occasionally or not at all. Another frequent location of L1 utterances was in instances of self-initiated self-repair (Schegloff, Jefferson, & Sacks, 1977). In cases of misspeaking speakers often lapsed into L1 to initiate the repair and then carried out the repair in L2 as illustrated below.

Excerpt 5
AEII Pre 0066

```
01. Ren: Tomorrow is Ryouya's tanjyoubi eh. tanjyoubi
02.      jyanai, >birthday birthday<
```

In this case, the speaker is talking about upcoming social plans, referring to his friend Ryouya's birthday. He misspeaks and uses the Japanese word for birthday (*tanjyoubi*). Realizing he has misspoken, he immediately initiates repair with the interjection 'eh' and then states in Japanese 'tanjyoubi jyanai', literally, 'no, not tanjyoubi'. He then completes the repair by supplying the correct English word 'birthday' twice in quick succession.

Excerpt 6
AEI Pre 0068

```
01. Mayu: Last year I visitedu Tsutenkaku first time
02. Kana: [Ha hah huhh ]
03. Mayu: [Ha hhh ha hh]
04. Kana: Me too >eh< me too jyanai I visited Tsutenkaku
05.       (2.1)
06.       eh In January.
```

In this excerpt speaker Mayu reports a visit to a well-known landmark the previous year. Kana offers an aligning utterance but immediately initiates repair. In this case the repairable item is not an L1 utterance but a factually incorrect utterance. The speaker, adhering to the Gricean maxim of truthfulness, wishes to state that she visited the landmark for the first time not last year, but in January of this year. The repair in this case is carried out with a repeat of the trouble source utterance ('*me too*'), which is negated by the L1 expression 'jyanai', ('*No*', or '*Not that*') and then the repair is completed.

Another aspect of repair that was widespread across speakers was the practice of multiple turn re-starts to repair items, even if the repairable items were not turn initial and the repairable item did not seem to pose any problem for the interlocutors' comprehension. The practice is illustrated in the following excerpt.

Excerpt 7
AEI Pre 0001

```
01. Mayu: Did you(.)give(.)[present to] your mother?
02. Yuka:                   [ah::::::::]
03.       Yes(.)ah:: I. I give. I gave(.)I gave flower
```

Yuka responds to a question with multiple restarts, progressing the turn by one-word increments. This kind of multiple restart and progress through the turn by one-word increments was common. The kind of things treated as repairable were such items as verb tense, word order and L1 utterances. Missing articles or absence of plural or third person singular suffixes were generally not noticed or oriented to as repairable.

Sequence Structure

Adjacency pairs are the central underlying structures of talk-in-interaction (Sacks, Schegloff, & Jefferson, 1974) and a canonical adjacency pair is the question followed by an answer (or an account of why no answer is forthcoming). Although mundane conversation may contain frequent questions and answers, it is obvious that this sequence structure cannot comprise the entirety of any extended social interaction. Such a mono-practice would be more representative of an interview genre, or classroom interaction.

Despite the genre inappropriateness of extended Q&A sequences in conversation, many of the *Pre* conversations featured such sequences. Firstly, questions were posed by one speaker. The questions were generally unelaborated, and comprised the entirety of a turn. Secondly, the answer to the question was similarly unelaborated, answering the question in minimalistic terms. The following excerpts are illustrative.

Excerpt 8
AEI Pre 0001

```
01. Yuka:   Whato (1.1) did you: (1.0) do?
02.         (2.1)
03.         weekend this (0.9) last weekend? weekend
04.         (4.8)
05. Mina:   >Part time job<
06. Yuka:   Oh? eh what whato what job?
07. Mina:   Conbini (.) ence store
08. Yuka:   Eh:: where? where?
```

09.   (1.9)
10. Mina: Near (.) my home.
11. Yuka: My home? (1.0)°my° near
12. Mina: Near.
13. Yuka: Near eh? Seven Eleven?
14. Mina: No circle K?
15. Yuka: Circle K? Circle K Circle K ah ah ah:::
16. Mina: Schoolu
17. Yuka: Ok ok oh eh::: (3.6) oh eh what time. (.) uh::
18.   (2.5)
19. Mina: Four ah four hours
20. Yuka: Four hours?

In this sequence, speaker Yuka poses a series of questions to Mina. The questions are all stand-alone and Yuka does not offer any kind of commentary to her questions or any kind of assessment to Mina's answers. Mina replies in a similarly minimalized fashion.

Excerpt 9
AE1 Pre 0005

01. T: I went to::: eh spring vacation I went to
02.   Tokyo
03. Y: Yeah.
04.   (0.8)
05. T: >n. de< I (.) I take=
06. Y: =You take
07. T: Ah. Earthquake=

08. Y: =You take earthquake?
09.   (3.9)
10. Y: what happened, eh, eh?
11. T: Every train stop.
12. Y: Oh
13. T: Taihendatta
14. Y: Eh you. you had very (.)very tired.
15. T: Yeah
16. Y: The(.)the earthquake opened o.er the
17.   earthquake often occurred
18. T: Occurred, occurred. Ueno Dobutsu en
19. Y: Oh. Ueno dobutsu en
20. T: Yes
21. Y: Eh.(1.1)Eh: What magnitude?
22. T: uh magnitude is Kyu ((nine))
23. Y: Ah, nine
24. T: Nine
25. Y: Nine
26. T: Oh nine

In this excerpt, T is recounting a trip to Tokyo during which there was an earthquake. Y asks for elaboration in line 04. 'What happened?' T responds by reporting that all trains stopped. This is receipted by Y and T offers the assessment in Japanese *'taihendatta'* (it was terrible). Y's next contribution seems to comment on the frequency of earthquakes and is possibly framed around the desire to use the word 'occurred'. In line 18 T interprets Y's comment as asking for his location at the time the earthquake struck, which he supplies by naming the location (Ueno zoo). No further elaboration of the precise nature of events is offered or sought following this. Y then moves forward by asking the magnitude of the earthquake. T responds by giving the magnitude in L1 (*Kyu*, i.e. nine). This becomes the focus for repair by Y. This sequence also demonstrated minimalized questions (*what happened*, line 10 and *what magnitude*, line 21) and minimalized answers (*every train stop*, line 11, *Ueno Dobutsuen*, line 18 and *magnitude is kyu*, line 22). Despite the high tellability inherent in a narrative concerning experiencing a major earthquake, both participants orient to a minimalized Q&A structure that does not really exploit the tellability of the material.

Receipt through Repetition

Excerpt 9 also shows another common feature of learner talk; receipt through repetition. The reasons that speakers may repeat their own or each other's words are multiple and varied (see Tannen, 2007). Of course, native speakers of English may receipt an utterance by repetition, so the practice in learner talk is not aberrant per se. Rather, its frequency in leaner talk may be an issue. Greer, Bussinguer, Butterfield, & Mischinger (2009, p. 25) note that "[...] too many of these sorts of repetitions might make talk seem unnatural ... " and in the case of Japanese learners, the practice may reflect a transfer from L1 interactions (see Campbell-Larsen, 2016). The receipt repetitions in lines 08, 18, and 23 - 26, and those in Excerpt 8 (lines 11, 12 and 15) give some flavor of the nature of repetition that often occurred in learner talk.

Vague Category Markers

Analysis of the *Pre* recordings showed several other recurrent pragmatic features. There was the absence of expressions that are termed Vague Category Markers (Evison, McCarthy, & O'Keeffe, 2007). There are expressions such as *and stuff like that; and those guys;* et cetera. They indicate epistemic convergence and also serve local, interactional functions. McCarthy (2010, p. 8) notes the occurrence of these items proximal to speaker transition, suggesting that they may serve as triggers for such transitions, and Evison, McCarthy and O'Keeffe (2007, p. 139) refer to the way in which these expressions "evoke and promote the active cooperation of the listener."

As Pekarek Doehler and Pochon-Berger (2011) point out, the use or nonuse of a particular interactional strategy is highly context dependent, so no definite statement can be made regarding learner competence in the case of non-occurrence. Participants may opt not to use an interactional strategy rather than be unable to. Nevertheless, the absence of general extenders across all of the *Pre* conversations is noticeable, as in the following excerpt.

Excerpt 10
AEI Pre 0004
```
01. Rina: What kind of job (.) what °do you° will
02.       you:: have part time job
03. Chie: Uh::I want to(.) some(.)café
04.       (6.0)
05.       I(1.6)don't don't decide a (1.0) °uh?°
06.       I don't decide ah (2.9) café eh?
```

In this excerpt Rina asks Chie what kind of part-time job she is looking for and Chie answers that she would like to work in '*some café*'. This would seem to be an excellent place to utter a general extender such as 'or something like that' or add another two items to create a three-part list (see Jefferson, 1990) both strategies serving as marker of possible turn completion. The silence in line 04 indicates some perturbation in the turn taking system. The absence of a pragmatic phenomenon is not evidence that a speaker is ignorant or unable to deploy it, but the absence of vague category markers across all *Pre* conversations is noted, even though there were ample opportunities for just this type of utterance.

Summary

The *Pre* recordings contained several recurrent points in learner speaking which can be broadly categorized as pragmatic in nature rather than grammatical or lexical. The overall structure of the interactions often followed a Q&A format with minimized questions and answers. Common English discourse markers were almost completely absent. L1 use was frequent and often systematic, with repeated use of L1 DM, reversion to L1 for repair and use of *aizuchi*-type responses. Use of repetition to receipt utterances was also widespread. Although some of the difficulties faced by the students could be ascribed to vocabulary and grammar difficulties and perhaps some lack of intimacy between speakers, these pragmatic points were notable.

The Classroom as a Social-Interactional Space

Following analysis of the *Pre* recordings, steps were taken to address some of the pragmatic aspects of learners' speaking. Before specific lesson plans could be implemented, the classroom had to be reorganized as an interactional space. The common concept of language classrooms in institutional settings is of a place that psychologically 'belongs' to the teacher and in which the students are passive recipients of knowledge disbursed by the teacher. Student speaking takes place under the direction of the teacher and is deemed legitimate only if it is in accordance with the teacher's institutional goals. Thus, student speaking often takes the form of classroom exchange described by Sinclair and Coulthard (1975). Student to student speaking, when it occurs, is usually goal oriented and typified by 'find someone who ...' type mixer activities, 'now ask your partner' prompts in textbooks, or the like. These phases of talk are initiated (and terminated) by the teacher, are mono-topical and are understood to be open to evaluation by the teacher. This is in contrast to mundane daily conversation which Nunan (1987, p. 137) describes thus:

> ... genuine communication is characterized by the uneven distribution of information, the negotiation of meaning (through for example, clarification requests and confirmation checks), topic nomination and negotiation by more than one speaker, and the right of interlocutors to decide whether to contribute to an interaction or not. In other words, in genuine communication, decisions about who says what to whom and when are up for grabs.

These aspects of conversation do not conform to student expectations of the kinds of speaking that normally take place in language classrooms in the Japanese context. Miller (1995) outlines differences between 'Western' and 'Japanese' communicative styles and proposes a 'Japanese-friendly' approach to language teaching (p. 46), but his suggestions are all still firmly within the realm of institutional talk. The conflict between institutional talk as the only kind of legitimate talk in L2 classrooms and social, participant-centered and managed talk is referenced by Seedhouse (2004) who argues that "... it is, in theory, not possible for L2 teachers to replicate conversation (in its CA sense) in the L2 classroom as part of a lesson." (p. 69).

From the outset of the course the students were told that every lesson would feature a period of free conversation. The students were informed that the transition to this lesson phase (termed 'Student Talk Time' or STT) would be minimal. The teacher would not suggest topics, provide handouts or other materials, select groups, set a time limit or delineate some goal to be achieved. The learners had to self-organize into speaking groups, initiate the conversation, nominate topics, manage turn taking, sustain progressivity and so on. All of these acts are central to participation in conversation, but normal teaching practice, even in so-called 'communicative language teaching' lessons often denies learners any agency in these matters. It is not surprising if students, habituated to such lack of agency, subsequently find it problematical to engage in conversation.

It is vital that students be made aware of the purposes of this phase and not misinterpret it as aimless filler. "Telling students about the aim(s) of a particular activity helps them to identify with these aims and hence feel more responsible for the outcome." (Scharle & Szabo, 2008, p. 8) During STT the teacher moved from group to group, sometimes joining in as a co-participant, sometimes monitoring, sometimes sitting with one group whilst directing attention towards another group in surreptitious monitoring, occasionally interrupting to suggest discourse marker use would be appropriate or highlighting L1 style backchannels or repair practices that were taking place. The STT phase usually lasted up to 40 minutes. This extensive period was deemed necessary as shorter periods seldom progressed past initial greetings and 'how was your weekend?' type exchanges and did not challenge the learners in terms of topic management and maintaining progressivity.

Even after explaining clearly the rationale behind the STT lesson phase, it took some period of weeks before students could engage in phatic talk. This is in all likelihood due to the task of overcoming deeply held views about what should and should not happen in a classroom inherited from previous experiences of institutional education. Early instances of STT featured frequent lapses in to silence, reversion to L1 or appeals to the teacher to supply a topic. However, the learners gradually oriented to this interactionally reconfigured classroom. L1 utterances decreased and some student groups even refused to allow the teacher to participate in ongoing conversations citing privacy and 'girls/boys talk' as reasons for the teacher to leave them alone to continue their interactions. This suspension of the teacher's right to enter learner interactions was a powerful indicator of the reconfigured nature of the psycho-social classroom space.

Teaching in Response to Data Analysis

The institution of STT was predicated on the idea that it had to be a feature of every lesson for it to be effective, rather than an occasional activity. A similar view was taken with the pragmatic issues identified in the analysis of the video data. For example, the concept of discourse markers was introduced early in the course. Videos of English native speaker interactions were shown which highlighted naturalistic DM use and gave students an awareness of the frequency, functions and prosody of English DM. Videos of Japanese interactions were also shown to raise awareness of the nature of DM in Japanese. The teacher modelled the use of DM in both Japanese and

English by making marked and unmarked responses to a question. The students were asked to evaluate which answer, marked or unmarked, was more fluent. The marked answer was judged a better response by all students. The learners were also shown their own *Pre* videos and directed to notice the lack of DM and the other phenomena discussed above.

Similar awareness raising activities were carried out with the other points noticed in the *Pre* videos such as *aizuchi* and backchannels, minimized questions and responses, vague category markers and so on. The following excerpt gives a flavor of the kind of speaking activities (outside STT) that occurred in later lessons. The overt target of the activity was to give hedged answers that were purposefully vague and used vague category markers.

Excerpt 11
OCII

```
01. S1:   What time do you usually go to bed on weekends?
02.       Eleven o'clock or twelve o'clock or something
03.       like that?
04. S2:   About one one thirty something like that
05. S1:   Oh great.
06. S1:   [Laughs]
07. S2:   [Laughs]
08. T:    Ok a:nd (.) you forgot the discourse marker
09.       We::ll
10. S2:   Ah:: [Matta] ((Oh Again))
11. T:         [Okay ] one more time
((Lines omitted))
```

```
12. T:      Okay same question, this time use a discourse
13.         marker in your answer yeah?
            ((Lines omitted))
14. S1:     What time do you usually go to bed on weekends?
15.         Eleven o'clock twelve o'clock and so on?
16. S2:     I mean [about ]
17. T:             [Uh uh↓]We::ll Ha ha OK. One more time
18.         question. start with well yeah okay? So and
19.         because she gave you a time but it's not your
20.         time you can say well actually=
21. S2:     =Oh
            ((Lines omitted))
22. T:      Okay right one more time. Question.
23. S1:     What time do you usually go to bed on weekends?
24.         Eleven o'clock, twelve o'clock something like
25.         that?
26. S2:     Well actually about one or one thirty something
27.         like that.
```

In this case the question is posed with exemplar answers embedded in the question rather than a minimized interrogative as was typical of *Pre conversations*. The answer is given in a vague way in line 04, aligning with the overt purpose of the activity. The teacher then offers a minimal positive assessment of this before pointing out that the interaction lacked discourse markers, and suggesting that the marker *well* would have been appropriate. The teacher then instructs the students in lines 12 and 13 to repeat the activity, but this time S2 should use a DM in her answer. After some meta-talk in Japanese (not included here) the students then re-start. This time S1 switches the general extender deployed at the end of the question from 'something like that', which was used in the first iteration of the question, to '*and so on*'. S2 responds with the DM *I mean*. The teacher interrupts this utterance suggesting *well* as a more canonical turn opener, especially I this case where the answer is subtly non-aligned with the answer projected by the question (see Heritage, 2015 and Schegloff & Lerner, 2009). The teacher also suggests that *actually* may also be appropriate here, indicating that S2 recognizes that some expectations were implicit in S1's question but these expectations have not been met. The teacher also comments that *and so on* is more commonly used in writing and that *something like that* is more appropriate to this conversation genre. The students then re-do the speaking activity, using the suggested language in a fluent and largely naturalistic manner.

This sequence illustrates the kinds of multi-focused and interventionist classroom speaking activities that occurred regularly in the lessons apart from the STT phase. Even though the overt target of the activity was to practice giving purposefully vague answers to questions, other issues such as embedding possible candidate answers into the question to support comprehensibility or signal expectations, and use of turn opening discourse markers and general extenders were also addressed.

This kind of intervention by the teacher also occurred in STT phases of the lessons. During ongoing interactions in which the teacher was variously a ratified participant, a non-participating but recognized over-hearer or an eavesdropper, the teacher would occasionally interject with brief statements concerning pragmatic aspects of talk, such as using appropriate DM, highlighting *aizuchi* utterances, completing turns with general extenders and other such practices. These interventions were designedly brief and produced to interfere with the progressivity of the interactions as little as possible. Given the re-configuration of the classroom as a social-interactive space mentioned above, this reversion to institutional concerns was minimized and replicated the ways in which brief episodes of 'attending to business' can occur in all conversations. Reversion to purely social interaction occurred unproblematically. Gradually, the mere presence of the teacher in proximity to ongoing student interactions prompted use of the pragmatic language, initially in a self-conscious and slightly labored way, but gradually moving to a more habitual and unselfconscious mode of expression.

Post and *Final* Conversations: Analysis and Change

Analysis of the *Post* and *Final* recordings showed broad, but uneven, uptake of the explicit language points and interactional behaviors taught during the course. Generally, the interactions featured less pausing, less L1 code switching, fewer instances of L1 DM and *aizuchi*-style listener responses. There were fewer extended sequences of minimized Q&A adjacency pairs. Questions were often elaborated and the responses to those questions were expanded and subject to commentary and evaluation in a way that supported progressivity. In the *Pre* recordings common English discourse markers were almost entirely absent. In the *Final* recordings DM usage was widespread and largely naturalistic, although there was variation across speakers. The types of sequence structure were more varied with fewer minimized question and answer sequences, questions being more supported with surrounding commentary and answers being expanded in ways that sustained progressivity. Other aspects of pragmatic language that were absent from the *Pre* conversations, such as upgrade adjectives in assessments, speedily concluded repairs and vague category markers were also present to greater or lesser extents in the learners' *Post* and *Final* conversations.

The following excerpt is illustrative. (These are the same speakers from excerpt 10.)

Excerpt 12
AEI Final 0061

```
01. Chie: Oh Rina today i:s ve- absolutely freezing
02. Rina: Yeah I think so you know but I like ah this
03.       weather but because I like it
04.       snow I want it to snow lots of do you think so=
05. Chie: =>yeah yeah yeah yeah< I think so oh actually I
06.       wi- I I'm going to::
07.       snowboarding in February=
08. Rina: =Oh nice
09. Chie: with my boyfriend=
10. Rina: =Yeah yeah yeah=
11. Chie: =So you you know >I mean< I maybe I will go::
12.       >Akakura Onsen[shiki< area]
13. Rina:            [°yeah yeah°]
14. Chie: Do you know >Akakura Onsen< oh >have you ever
15.       been to< snowboarding or skiing
16. Rina: Well I don't know Akakura Onse[n    ]
17. Chie:                               [Yeah]
18. Rina: but I'm:: I want to go snowboarding
19. Chie: Yeah. Ye[ah  ]
```

```
20. Rina:         [may]I mean ah:: maybe I will go to
21.      snowboarding
22. Chie: Oh=
23. Rina: =in February=
24. Chie: =Wow=
25. Rina: =with my friend so ahm >you know< (.)I don't (.)
26.      I haven't never go been to snowboarding=
```

In this case, the speakers engage each other in a much more sophisticated manner than was the case in the *Pre* conversation. There are multiple instances of fluent DM usage, (lines 05, 11, 16, 20 and 25), turn transition is carried out without pausing, there are no instances of L1 usage, self-initiated self-repair is carried out swiftly, (E.g. line 01, 06, 18) naturalistic L2 backchannels abound (lines 08, 10, 13, 17, 19, 22, 24) and speaker C uses an upgrade adjective with its appropriate intensifier in line 01.

As mentioned above, many of the features of the learner talk in the *Pre* recordings were highly individuated. In excerpt 2 Kana's talk was marked by distinctive *aizuchi* responses. In the *Final* recordings her responses were recognizably in English (*yeah, uh huh, I see*). Speaker Mayu from excerpt 3, had talk in the *Pre* recordings that was heavily marked in L1 DMs (usually *etoh*). In the *Final* recording this speaker had zero instances of this word or any other L1 markers.

Even students who made much less progress in their speaking still showed some recognizable orientation towards a more interactive style of speaking. Speaker A in excerpt 4 had talk that was replete with pauses, L1 utterances, grammatical infelicities and general problems with turn taking in both *Pre* and *Final* recordings. However, closer examination reveals some more nuanced practices.

Excerpt 13
AEIII Final 1:12
```
01. B: What will you have (0.5) spring vacation plan
02. A: yeah I spring vacation (.) plan (2.1) ye. parttime
03.    job member in (.) is eh sportchie
04. B: Oh
05. A: Basketball eh (.) Volleyball eh (1.0) tennis (1.0)
06.    something like that)
07. B: S::: huh hh. hh.
08.    (2.7)
09. A: You know?
```

In this case A mentions his part-time job in a sports club ('*sportchie*') and illustrates with a three-part list. He concludes this list with a general extender ('*something like that*') apparently to indicate a complete turn. B does not take a subsequent turn and a pause of 2.7 seconds occurs. A then re-signals his orientation to speaker transition by using the marker *You know* in line 09. Despite the multiple and extended pauses and grammatical infelicities, A seems to orient (at least some extent) towards managing turn-taking and progressivity.

Discussion

Learning a foreign language in a formal institutional context presents many challenges to learners and teachers alike. The central use of language is spoken language, especially mundane social interaction, i.e. conversation.

When we ask about a person's abilities in a foreign language, we ask *Do you speak English/ German/ French,* etc. However, spontaneous spoken interaction does not lend itself well to the exigencies of institutional learning. Strict adherence to utterances that would pass muster as written language is not the norm in spontaneous spoken interaction. Problems with speaking, hearing and understanding are commonplace even in native speaker talk and comprehensibility is often arrived at after interactants work together to create shared understanding. This intersubjectivity is at odds with the individualized performance evaluations that apply in most formal educational contexts.

Many of the means by which spontaneous spoken interaction proceeds are not available to the intuition of speakers and may even be stigmatized (see Campbell-Larsen, 2017) and pushed to the periphery in syllabi. This paper has suggested that for learners to move towards more accomplished pragmatic performance in the L2 several things need to be in place. Firstly, teachers must have a clear understanding of the importance and nature of spoken interaction and communicate this to students. Secondly, a small number of pragmatic language items such as DMs, backchannels, general extenders, repair strategies and the like should be repeatedly taught and form a background to all speaking activities, whatever the current target. Thirdly, teachers must have the ability to identify highly individuated pragmatic behavior such as reliance on L1 backchannels or orientation to a Q+A style of interaction. Fourthly, students should be habituated to regular periods of spontaneous, autonomous, spoken interaction, i.e. conversation, in the L2. By these means learners can be made aware of the particular L2 pragmatic resources that are available to speakers and also of their own individual traits and behaviors. The combination of explicit teaching with extensive opportunity to engage in spontaneous interaction with minimal interference from the teacher gradually leads to more nuanced and varied modes of spoken interaction. The last word goes to a student who agreed to be interviewed regarding the contents and methodology of the course.

'It's not just wasting a time. You give us a really efficient way to improve our conversational ability. Also it's not just like a writing conversation I mean it's not only textbook it's like right or I see and it's like you know discourse. We can improve how to behave in the conversation.'

References

Campbell-Larsen, J. (2017). Discourse markers in the classroom. In P. Clements, A. Krause, & H. Brown (Eds.), *Transformation in language education* (pp. 227-234). Tokyo, Japan: JALT.

Campbell-Larsen, J. (2016). I think so too: Assessments and agreements. In P. Clements, A. Krause, & H. Brown (Eds.), *Focus on the learner* (pp. 225-231). Tokyo, Japan: JALT.

Clancy, P. M., Thompson, S. A., Suzuki, R., & Tao, H. (1996). The conversational use of reactive tokens in English, Japanese, and Mandarin. *Journal of Pragmatics, 26*(3), 355-387.

Dwyer, E., & Heller-Murphy, A. (1996). Japanese learners in speaking classes. *Edinburgh Working Papers in Applied Linguistics, 7*, 46-55.

Ellis, R. (1991). Communicative competence and the Japanese learner. *JALT Journal, 13*(2), 103-129.

Evison, J., McCarthy, M., & O'Keeffe, A. (2007). 'Looking out for love and all the rest of it': Vague category markers as shared social space. In J. Cutting (Ed.), *Vague language explored* (pp. 138-157). Basingstoke, England: Palgrave Macmillan.

Greer, T., Bussinguer, V., Butterfield, J., & Mischinger, A. (2009). Receipt through repetition. *JALT Journal, 31*(1), 5-34.

Heritage, J. (2015). Well-prefaced turns in English conversation: A conversation analytic perspective. *Journal of Pragmatics, 88*, 88-104.

Jefferson, G. (1990). List construction as a task and interactional resource. In G. Psathas, (Ed.), *Interactional competence* (pp. 63-92). Lanham, MD: University Press of America.

LoCastro, V. (1987). Aizuchi: A Japanese conversational routine. In L. E. Smith (Ed.), *Discourse across cultures: Strategies in world Englishes* (pp. 101-113). London, England: Prentice Hall.

McCarthy, M. (2010). Spoken fluency revisited. *English Profile Journal, 1*(1), 1-15.

Miller, T. (1995). Japanese learners' reactions to communicative English lessons. *JALT Journal, 17* (1), 31-49.

Nunan, D. (1987). Communicative language teaching: Making it work. *ELT journal, 41*(2), 136-145.

Pekarek Doehler, S., & Pochon-Berger, E. (2011). Developing "methods" for interaction: a cross-sectional study of disagreement sequences in French L2. In J. K. Hall, J. Hellermann, & S. Pekarek Doehler (Eds.), *L2 interactional competence and development* (pp. 206-243). Bristol, England: Multilingual Matters.

Pritchard, R. M., & Maki, H. (2006). The changing self-perceptions of Japanese university students of English. *Journal of Studies in International Education, 10*(2), 141-156.

Psathas, G., & Anderson, T. (1990). The 'practices' of transcription in conversation analysis. *Semiotica, 78*(1-2), 75-100.

Sacks, H., Schegloff, E. A., & Jefferson, G. (1974). The simplest systematics for the organization of turn-taking for conversations. *Language, 50*(4), 696-735.

Scharle, A., & Szabo, S. (2000). *Learner autonomy. A guide to developing learner responsibility.* Cambridge, England: Cambridge University Press.

Schegloff, E. A., & Lerner, G. H. (2009). Beginning to respond: Well-prefaced responses to wh-questions. *Research on Language and Social Interaction, 42,* 91-115.

Schegloff, E. A., Jefferson, G., & Sacks, H. (1977). The preference for self-correction in the organization of repair in conversation. *Language, 53,* 361-382.

Seedhouse, P. (2004). *The interactional architecture of the language classroom: A conversation analysis perspective.* Oxford, England: Blackwell.

Sinclair, J. M., & Coulthard, M. (1975). *Towards an analysis of discourse: The English used by teachers and pupils.* Oxford, England: Oxford University Press.

Tannen, D. (2007). *Talking voices: Repetition, dialogue, and imagery in conversa-*

tional discourse (Vol. 26). Cambridge, England: Cambridge University Press.

Yngve, V. (1970). On getting a word in edgewise. In M.A Campbell (Ed.), *Papers from the Sixth Regional Meeting of the Chicago Linguistic Society* (pp. 567-577). Chicago, IL: Chicago Linguistic Society.

Appendix: Transcription Notations

Simultaneous utterances
I went [with my] friend   Left square brackets mark the start of overlapping talk
       [yeah   ]   Right square brackets mark the end of overlapping talk

Contiguous utterances
=   Equals signs show:
                      a) that talk is latched; that is there is no pause between the end of one turn and the start of the next turn
                      b) that a turn continues at the next equals sign on a subsequent line

Pauses
(0.6)   Numerals in parentheses show pauses in tenths of a second
(.)   A period in parentheses indicates a micropause

Characteristics of speech delivery
<u>Weekend</u>   Underlining indicates marked stress
Job?   A question mark indicates rising intonation
Finish.   A period indicates falling intonation
> you know<   Inward facing indents indicate talk which is faster than the surrounding talk
Ni:::ce   One or more colons indicates a lengthening of the preceding sound. More colons prolong the stretch
°nice°   Degree signs indicate speech that is quieter than the surrounding talk
NEVER   Capitals indicate speech that is louder than the surrounding talk

The Use of Spontaneous Gesture as a Multimodal Interactional Strategy in English as a Lingua Franca Interactions: The Case of Non-Understanding Sequences

Hiroki Hanamoto

Abstract

This study investigated the use of spontaneous gesture as a multimodal interactional strategy in English as a lingua franca (ELF) dyadic interactions. Four participants in a Japanese university context voluntarily participated in this study, in which two Japanese university students interacted with international students from Nepal and Indonesia. The non-understanding sequences in their multimodal interactions were transcribed and annotated using ELAN, an open-source software, and were analyzed using a multimodal analysis incorporating conversation analysis transcription conventions. Detailed analysis of the spontaneous gestures in their interactions showed that the speakers repeatedly and consistently used deictic and metaphoric gestures in their turn-taking as a cognitive and a communicative strategy to highlight spatial representation and enhance comprehension of their speech. In other words, the findings demonstrated interactional gestural alignment, suggesting that the interlocutors' interactions were mediated and assisted by gestures. The study's findings also imply that spontaneous gesture can be utilized as a valuable visual and interactional aid in

ELF interactions.

Keywords: spontaneous gesture, space representation, non-understanding, multimodality, ELF interaction

Introduction

Many studies have emphasized the important functions of non-verbal actions in enhancing successful interactive meaning construction in English as a lingua franca (henceforth, ELF) interactions (e.g., Kaur, 2011; Ke & Cahyani, 2014; Matsumoto, 2015). However, few studies considering body language and multimodality employed by ELF speakers when negotiating meaning have been conducted. According to Block (2014), gesture serves an essential function and is a significant way of communicating in spoken language. Therefore, by employing a multimodal analysis that incorporates conversation analysis transcription conventions, the present study examines spontaneous gesture sequences occurring when ELF speakers must address non-understanding. More specifically, the type and function of the use of hand gestures with speech produced by ELF speakers will be qualitatively analyzed.

Literature Review

This section begins with a review and the definition of ELF, and continues with a summary of the salient features of multimodal interaction. Then, a justification is offered for the integration of multimodal resources alongside language in the analysis. Next, we summarize studies where the focus has been on the importance of hand gestures in interactions. Finally, the research aim is outlined.

English as a Lingua Franca (ELF)

In light of the concept of World Englishes and ELF, which both refer to English being used between and/or among non-native English speakers, it is correct to suggest that the different varieties deserve to be recognized (e.g., Kachru, 1996) and that acquiring native-like competence is not always relevant for communication, but rather mutual intelligibility is the goal (e.g., Jenkins, 2006; Seidlhofer, 2011). What is certain is that for participants in ELF interactions, where English is not the primary language of their community, English is used as a contact or medium language and serves a means of communication. From these perspectives, one must consider that ELF speakers might enhance interactional communicative strategies that enable interlocutors from a wide range of disparate cultural and linguistic backgrounds to negotiate diversity in their interactions with one another.

Multimodal Interaction

Most previous ELF interaction studies have focused on linguistic verbal strategies in the case of incomprehension sequences (e.g., Cogo, 2010; Firth, 1996; Jenkins, 2006; Kaur, 2009). However, the objects and approaches of ELF interactions have gradually changed since the 2000s to include non-verbal semiotic resources (e.g., Goodwin, 2003; Kress, 2000; Leeuwen, 2005; Matsumoto, 2015).

To explain the mode as a means of multimodality in communication, Block (2014, p. 61) cited Gee (2011) to describe how speakers show their identities and engage in activities not only using language, but also by "using language together with other 'stuff' that isn't language." In other words, modes such as proxemics, posture, gesture, and body movements, according to Block, seem to serve an essential function in ELF communication and represent a significant method of enhancing spoken interactions.

Summarizing the discussions of existing multimodality research (e.g., Block, 2014; Jewitt, 2009; Kress, 2000; Stam & McCafferty, 2008; Stein & Newfield, 2006), research incorporating other modes in addition to language during meaning negotiation in incomprehension sequences is still in its infancy (e.g., Canagarajah, 2013; Matsumoto, 2015; Stein & Newfield, 2006), especially the study of multimodal resources including hand gestures. Therefore, the use of body language and multimodality in ELF interactions require further research attention.

The Use of Gesture in Interactions

Intentionally or not, we use gesture as well as linguistic resources in interactions (Goodwin, 2003), which all serve in the process of mutual understanding. Kita (2000) identified two possible reasons why speakers use gestures: to convey messages to an interlocutor and to facilitate speech production. In other words, in the former case, a speaker uses gestures in communication to benefit the listener, while the latter benefits the speaker's own cognitive processes. Accordingly, gestures are an integral communicative resource performed by both speakers and listeners.

As far as gestures are concerned, it is important to note the relationship between gesture and speech. To begin with, in terms of communicative perspective, gesture and speech seem to be tightly interconnected (e.g., Kendon, 2004). According to McNeill (1992, 2005), gestures generally occur synchronously with, or slightly before, the onset of speech, namely spontaneous gesture, although sometimes gestures are used without any accompanying speech. This is in keeping with the finding of Gullberg (1998), which is that gesture production tends to cease when speech ceases. Thus, it is not surprising that the meaning and function of gesture are dependent on the accompanying speech and context.

Spontaneous Gesture for Establishing Intersubjectivity

Although gestures have undoubtedly communicative functions, there are a few different types of spontaneous gestures (McNeill, 1992, 2005). According to McNeill, there are four kinds of gestures recognized in the literature: iconics ("gestures that simulate movements or objects"), metaphorics ("imagistic representation of abstract ideas"), deictics ("pointing at objects"), and beats ("abrupt up-and-down movement of fingers or hands") (Lantolf & Thorne, 2006, p. 95). It is interesting to note that gesticulation is useful in understanding the relationship between gesture and speech, and has shed more light on spontaneous gesture production, although this gesticulation is in fact not always divided, since gestures have multiple functions (McNeill, 2005).

It has also been found that spontaneous gestures express variation in meaning and function, intrapersonally (cognitive function) and interpersonally (communicative function) (Galati & Brennan, 2014). Concerning their cognitive function, gestures can facilitate speakers' cognitive processes and production (e.g., Kita, 2000; McNeill & Duncan, 2000), and are important for encoding and decoding the messages that a speaker wishes to convey to an interlocutor (e.g., Tuite, 1993). This is not surprisingly because, in most spoken interactions, the frequency of spontaneous gesture use among speakers is much higher than among listeners. In other words, we can conclude that gestural production is a speaker-oriented action rather than a listener-oriented action (Tuite, 1993).

In terms of the communicative function of gesture, on the other hand, spontaneous gestures allow speakers to process messages more efficiently. Antes (1996) demonstrated that speakers in interactions employ spontaneous gestures as a repair strategy in sequential turns such as clarification requests, repetition, paraphrasing, and for solving problematic situations, while several other studies have shown that spontaneous gestures seem to function as a means of accommodation (e.g., Giles & Smith, 1979), enhancing explicitness (e.g., Kendon, 2004; McNeill & Duncan, 2000), turn-taking (e.g., Duncan, 1972), and achieving alignment through gestural catchment (e.g., McNeill, 2005). In other words, gesture can be used as a strategy to highlight the communicative relevance of establishing intersubjectivity.

Spontaneous gestural behavior between speakers and listeners is therefore relevant in the study of face-to-face interactions. In the case of ELF interaction, in which the first languages of the speakers are different, however, gestural behavior is relevant in developing and enhancing interactional communication strategies in making the effort to communicate between/among the participants while ensuring mutual understanding. However, as mentioned above, although ELF research integrating gesture resources into analyses has been increasing, the subject still requires further explanation. Moreover, many previous studies on gesture have been conducted from a psychological cognitive perspective (e.g., Kita, 2000; McNeill & Duncan, 2000; Tuite, 1993). Much less research, therefore, has addressed how interlocutors employ spontaneous gestures interpersonally in non-understanding sequences. The present study, therefore, examines spontaneous gesture sequences used by ELF speakers when confronting situations of non-understanding and explains how they employ such gestures. Furthermore, the study elucidates the types and functions of spontaneous gestures produced when negotiating meaning to overcome non-understanding in informal paired ELF interactions.

Method

The data analyzed in this study were obtained from two video-recorded ELF conversational interactions in English involving four participants from three different first language and culture backgrounds.

Research Participants

There were four ELF users majoring in science and engineering in this study. They were all non-native English speakers, including two native Japanese speakers (Ten and Taka), one native Nepalese speaker (Pa), and one native Indonesian speaker (Au). All participant names mentioned in this study are pseudonyms. They all attended mandatory English as a foreign language classes, which were approximately intermediate-level according to a TOEIC-based measurement. As the data for this study consisted of naturally occurring face-to-face interactions, it is difficult to report each participant's oral English proficiency level beyond that of their English class. Thus, following the class guideline, the author judged their oral English proficiency level to be in the intermediate range. The research participants' attributes, including gender, first language (L1), relationship with one another, and English proficiency level are described in Table 1.

Procedure

Upon receiving informed consent from the participants, the experiment was carried out in pairs. The participants came to the lab individually and

Table 1
Study Participant Information

Dyad	Name	L1	Relationship	English proficiency	Duration of recording (min:sec)
1	Ten (m)	Japanese	First meeting	Intermediate	18.51
	Pa (f)	Nepalese	First meeting	Intermediate	
2	Taka (m)	Japanese	First meeting	Intermediate	18.07
	Au (m)	Indonesian	First meeting	Intermediate	

were paired up for the videotaping of an approximately 15-minute natural conversation in English. A digital video camera with a microphone was set up to clearly capture the participants' simultaneous non-verbal actions and utterances. The participants did not know each other before the video-recording. They were encouraged to explore possible topics and talk freely about whatever topic they were interested in. To record their interaction as it occurred naturally and avoid the influence of the presence of the camera, the author left the lab, leaving the pairs alone, after they had started their conversations. Despite the interactions being recorded, as they progressed, each dyad's conversation seemed to develop into an authentic interaction.

Data Analysis

Most data analysis methods were based on talk-in-interaction (e.g., Schegloff, 2007) through multimodal repair sequences (Olsher, 2008) to understand the process of how ELF speakers co-create meaning through verbal utterances and accompanying gestures in incomprehension sequences. Selected excerpts from both video recordings were transcribed and analyzed using Jefferson's (1984) conversation analytic conventions and those of Mc-

Neill (2005) for non-verbal features (See Appendix A for more details).

For gesture analysis, based on McNeill (2005), hand gestures were classified into five categories: iconics, beats, metaphorics, deictics, and non-identifiable gestures, although the purpose of this study was not to codify gestures in a strict quantitative manner. Furthermore, ELAN, an open-source software, was used to annotate multimodal interaction and demonstrate gesture "strokes" (McNeill, 2005).

Concerning the process of sequences of non-understanding, based on Bremer (1996), the author defines non-understanding as that which occurs "when the listener realizes, that s/he cannot make sense of (part of) an utterance" (p. 40). The significant connotation here is that non-understanding is "a grader phenomenon" (p. 40) toward achieving mutual understanding.

Results and Discussion

Deictic and Metaphoric Gestures for Indicating Spatial Representation

The first excerpt is an example of a negotiation in which the participant addresses his interlocutor's problems in understanding using deictic and metaphoric gestures. Excerpt 1 is from the recorded corpus of Japanese male, Ten (T), and Nepalese female, Pa (P), who are talking about food. We can observe that the transversal gesture as well as the comparative gesture highlight the comparison. A multi-layered ELAN transcript of the interaction is provided in Figure 7.

Experts have illustrated how a speaker uses deictic and metaphoric gestures to indicate spatial representation (Kendon, 1990), specifically to compare countries along with two different perspectives, the comparative axis and the transversal axis. In line 1, Ten completes his turn, and in the fol-

Excerpt 1: "Nepalese kome" (from Dyad 1)

T (m) = Japanese; P (f) = Nepalese

```
 1.  T:  sushi rice is a little sweet.
 2.  P:  yeah: but different
 3.  T:  (2) un? ((moves his face closer to P))
→4.  P:  (.) bu:t good (.) and (.) {Nepalese.
                                 {((moves left hand toward space in front of her
→5.      chest and holds left hand pointing downward))
→6.
→7.      ko{me (rice)?
→8.        {((moves left hand up and holds left hand pointing downward))=
→9.  T:  ah:: ((nodding repeatedly))=
```

Figure 1 Nepalese *kome*.

→10. P: =rice?(.)and: {Japanese rice is::
→11.   {((moves right hand toward space in front of chest and holds
→12.   right hand pointing downward, still maintaining left hand pointing downward))

Figure 2 Japanese rice is.

lowing turn (line 2), Pa sets up an "adjacency pair" (Sacks, Schegloff, & Jefferson, 1974) through the continuer marker "yeah" (Heritage, 1984), and then utters that Japanese sushi rice is a little different from rice in her country, Nepal. Here, Ten addresses the problem segment through the minimal feedback token (Vasseur, Broeder, & Roberts, 1996) "un?", after a two-second pause with the display of a head movement. Thus, Pa's word "different" followed by the extended sound "yeah" could be identified as a "trigger" (Varonis & Gass, 1985) for attempting to open a repair space in the next action.

Pa uses deictic and metaphoric gestures, and her use of gestures in this section proceeds in two stages, the comparative axis, and the transversal axis, which is especially linked to the third spatial presentation. First, she uses a deictic gesture for the comparative axis perspective to compare Japan and Nepal. In fact, in lines 4-8 (Figure 1), she points her left hand to express Japanese rice, and when describing rice in Nepal, she uses her right hand to point (lines 10-12 and Figure 2). Pa's left hand gesture is synchronized with the phrase "Nepalese rice," while her right hand gesture precedes the phrase "Japanese rice is." Here, she employs a series of gestural movements to facilitate the interaction, and Pa's comparative pointing gestures specify the spatial position between Japan and Nepal explicitly.

After establishing alignment using Ten's minimal response token, Pa next attempts to employ some other gestures for the metaphorical representation of space. In line 14, Pa overtly moves to refer to the rice difference between Japan and Nepal, using transversal axis gestures. Clearly, in lines 14-15, Pa attempts to provide a detailed description of the rice difference between Japan and Nepal, by saying "really" with an extended sound. Here, she modifies the previous comparative gesture employed in lines 11-12 (Figure 2 in

Excerpt 2: "re::ally different from my country" (from Dyad 1)

```
13.    T:  oah:°((nodding repeatedly))
→14.   P:  re{::ally
→15.       {((moves both hands in parallel toward the space in front of her chest))
→16.       {different from (.) my country
→17.       {{((moves both hands apart laterally and moves both hands back in front of
→18.       her chest repeatedly))
```

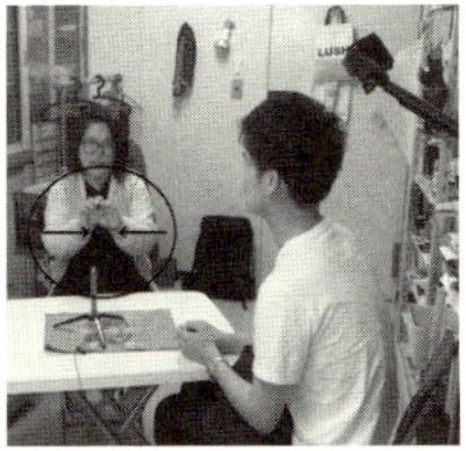

Figure 3
Really different (1).

Figure 4
Really different (2).

Figure 5
Really different (3).

Figure 6
Really different (4).

Figure 7   Multi-layered ELAN transcript, lines 4-18.

Excerpt 1), and moves to employ gestures to highlight the transversal axis. In other words, she concurrently employs both hands in a metaphoric gesture to indicate that there is a large difference in the way rice tastes in Japan and Nepal.

Figures 3-6 show how the gesture stroke is synchronized with co-verbal speech and highlights her intended meaning. Pa conveys the message "really" synchronized with the parallel movement of her hands in front of her chest. Then, she initiates the phrase "different from my country" by extending both hands laterally, and the shortening the distance between them. Interestingly, she repeatedly and consistently uses this transversal axis gesture during her speech. It is apparent that her series of gestures is intended to represent space. Thus, by producing her container gesture (McNeill, 1992) and spatial representation category (Kendon, 1990), her use of a transversal axis gesture seems to be intended as a spatial representation for Ten.

Achieving Alignment through Deictic Gestures

The next excerpt consists of a conversation between a Japanese male student, Taka (T), and an Indonesian male student, Au (A). Excerpt 3 is part of a conversation in which they are talking about the city where Taka was born. This excerpt captures how Au and Taka employ gestures for spatial representation, and achieve alignment through gestural catchment (e.g., McNeill, 2005).

In line 1, Au attempts to clarify the city where Taka was born, and Taka initiates a quick round of turn-taking by using the affirmative "yes," but also by nodding in both lines 3 and 4. In the turn that follows this (line 5), however, Au whispers the name of the city where Taka was born, because he is unfamiliar with the city. This is a strategic choice for expressing Au's clarification request to emphasize the information explicitly. Taka's repetition of other-speaker repetition (lines 6 and 7) in combination with the non-verbal action of "nodding" contributes to signaling agreement. It seems that Au's understanding and their quick negotiation of the sequence are successful at this point. Interestingly, we can see that Au again moves back to the spoken lexical item, and then modifies it, changing from the city name "Ogawa" to the station name "Ogawamachi" by himself (line 8). Following this, Taka quickly repeats the word as an instance of repetition, and, then also gives an example to Taka that Ogawamachi station is on the Tobu Tojyo Line. In other words, it appears that Au seems to be more familiar with the station name "Ogawamachi" than the city name "Ogawa."

Here, their collaborative interaction, in which they employ spontaneous gestures, is initiated immediately after this line. First, we can see Au showing his understanding of the previous turn overlapping with Taka's lines 10-11 by gesturing with his left hand. He moves his left index finger to point upward; however, this movement does not include any sign and indicates spatial representation (Figure 8). Rather, this "simple rhythmic gesture" (Gullberg, 1998, p. 94), beat, employed by Au seems to illustrate the communicative strategy as a display of understanding. Moreover, Au continues to engage in interaction using spontaneous gestures to fill in details. Specifically, we can see initially how Au achieves his alignment with Taka through the gestural catchment in lines 12-20. For instance, we can see that Au frequently attempts to use pointing gestures with his right index finger and hand to indicate direction and spatial representation. Interestingly, his right index finger gradually shifts into his right hand during the gesture

Excerpt 3: "Tobu line" (from Dyad 2)

T (m) = Japanese; A (m) = Indonesian

```
 1.  A: so you were born. in {this city?=
 2.                           {((moves left hand to point downward))
 3.  T:  ={yes
 4.       {((nodding))
 5.  A: °uhm Ogawa?°
 6.  T:  {Ogawa
 7.       {((nodding))
→8.  A: (.) Ogawamachi=
→9.  T: = Ogawamachi.ah::To{bu:[line
→10. A:                        [Tobu:s- ((moves left index finger to point
→11.                            upward))
```

Figure 8 Tobu line.

The Use of Spontaneous Gesture as a Multimodal Interactional Strategy in English as a Lingua Franca Interactions   215

→12. Tobu line: ((moves left hand down, and moves right index finger up to
→13.   point, then moves it down slowly to point to the left, and maintains it
→14.   until line 16;in this stroke he gradually shifts his right index finger
→15.   into his right hand to indicate the direction))
→16. T: (line. last. [station::
→17.   (((moves left hand up, then moves it down to point in the same direction that
→18.   A signals and slowly repeats this movement twice))
→19. A: [(last. - station (.) ah-ah-ah
→20.   (((maintains right hand pointing to the left))

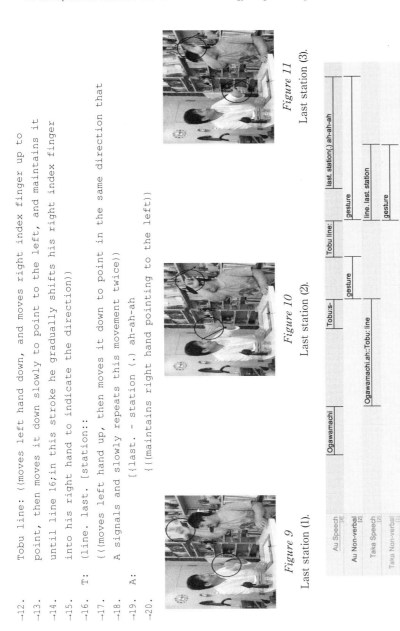

Figure 9
Last station (1).

Figure 10
Last station (2).

Figure 11
Last station (3).

Figure 12 Multi-layered transcript: lines 8-20.

Excerpt 4: "all the train go to" (from Dyad 2)

T (m) = Japanese; A (m) = Indonesian

```
1.   T:  {to Shinrinkouen (.) not. (.) Ogawa-town
2.        {((describes a route map on the paper and explains the route))
3.   A:  (2)((nodding repeatedly))
4.   T:  we:: {exchange [train
5.              {((makes circles with both hands in front of his chest and repeats
6.             this movement until line 7))
7.   A:                 [ah: I see I see I see
8.   T:  ah:=
→9.  A:  =all the {train. go to Shinrinkouen
→10.             {((moves both hands from his right side to center of his body to
→11.            indicate the spatial relationship))
```

Figure 13
All the train go to (1).

Figure 14
All the train go to (2).

Figure 15
All the train go to (3).

The Use of Spontaneous Gesture as a Multimodal Interactional Strategy in English as a Lingua Franca Interactions   217

```
12.  T:  ye[:s
→13. A:  [not (every train (.) go to Ogawa
→14.     (((begins to move both hands, which are maintained in the center of
→15.     his body, to his left side to indicate the spatial relationship, but more
→16.     widely and distantly from Au, compared to lines 9-11))
 17. T:  yeah yes yes=
 18. A:  =something like that? =
 19. T:  =((nodding repeatedly)
```

Figure 16
Every train go to (1).

Figure 17
Every train go to (2).

Figure 18
Every train go to (3).

Figure 19 Multi-layered transcript: lines 9-19.

stroke (McNeill, 2005) (lines 12-15). With this gesture, Au attempts to refer to the spatial position that he wants to describe explicitly. What is noteworthy here is that Taka is also employing and mimicking a similar gesture, gestural catchment, which Au gestures in the previous turn as a listener, and they each initiate negotiation for co-constructing spatial representation as "common ground" (Firth, 1996). Specifically, Au and Taka aligned with each other by employing a similar deictic gesture indicating spatial representation. In other words, their turn-taking through gestural catchment, in lines 8 and 20, shows their engagement leading to a successful communication outcome (Figures 9-11 and multi-layered ELAN transcript in Figure 12).

Later, Au and Taka talk about the location again. In their sequence, Au asks Taka how to get to Ogawamachi station, and they co-create meaning verbally and non-verbally, incorporating additional resources into their turns, such as using a route map to close the information gap and enhance communication. Au, at the end of the sequence, employs similar gestures indicating the metaphorical representation of space. Excerpt 4 displays another example of a participant employing gestures to indicate space to display his understanding and achieve interactional alignment between interlocutors.

This excerpt shows that Au and Taka are engaging in interaction toward the co-construction of meaning with the help of additional resources. Speech and non-verbal annotations are shown in Figure 19. We can initially find that Au frequently uses both hands to indicate spatial representation and express location in lines 9-11 and 13-16. However, each object he is referring to and gesture stroke are slightly distinctive. Here, he begins to move both hands from his right side to the center of his body (Figures 13-

15), on the other hand, he starts his hand movement from the front of his body, and moves both hands to the left side in lines 13-16 (Figures 16-18). Accordingly, it appears that he adapts his gesture depending on the context. Moreover, his gestures in lines 13-16 are more dynamic compared to lines 9-11, and seem to express that Ogawa is located far away from Shinrinkouen. The direction in which he moves both hands is not related to the actual location, but he assumes that it is metaphorically located somewhere "ahead" of Au and Taka. Thus, this analysis demonstrates that, through this style of interaction, they overcome the difficulties, and achieve interactional alignment by indicating spatial representation using gestures with speech.

Conclusion

The present study investigated how ELF speakers employ spontaneous gestures when dealing with instances of non-understanding, using (1) the video-recorded conversational data in naturally occurring face-to-face ELF interaction, and (2) a multimodal analysis incorporating conversation analysis transcription conventions. By combining multimodal repair sequences (Olsher, 2008) and Bremer's non-understanding framework (1996), the present study identified a "trigger" (Varonis & Gass, 1985) for the negotiation of meaning to resolve the issues of employing gestures.

The results showed that the trigger that the participants needed to employ spontaneous gestures was not meant to overcome difficulties in verbal expression but rather to enhance explicitness. In fact, the participants in this study gestured with both hands to accompany speech to represent spatial positioning and the metaphorical presentation of space in their minds. Based on the analysis, the gestures employed by the participants helped clarify their utterances in the sequence and improve intelligibility for their interlocutor. We can see here that using some types of gestures, namely deictic and metaphoric gestures, in combination with speech allowed the interlocutors to relieve tension and negotiate the lack of understanding, as well as to facilitate the cognitive processes of the speakers. Thus, this implies that understanding gestures help us understand what is actually going on in the interaction, even when we face difficulties ourselves verbally. Thus, employing gesture is a useful way of co-constructing meaning and achieving interactional alignment with an interlocutor.

The present study conducted an in-depth analysis of ELF face-to-face interactions and negotiation of meaning for co-constructing meaning using spontaneous gestures while dealing with problems in understanding. When speakers are engaged in ELF interactions, as they are exposed to different varieties of English, they use and rely on gestures, and convey messages verbally and nonverbally during interaction. The findings of this study suggest important implications concerning enhancing interactional communication strategies and emphasizing the important function of gestures in speech (e.g., Gullberg, 1998; McNeill, 2005). This study suggests the need to raise awareness of the importance of gesture use in ELF interactions, as well as the importance of gesture in understanding the process through which ELF speakers construct and achieve interactional alignment with an interlocutor.

Acknowledgements

The author is grateful to Lala U. Takeda and Megumi Okugiri for this opportunity. The author would also like to thank the anonymous reviewers for their constructive comments on an earlier draft of this paper. Finally, the author would like to thank the four participants of this study.

References

Antes, T. A. (1996). Kinesics: The value of gesture in language and in the language classroom. *Foreign Language Annals, 29*, 439-448. doi:10.1111/j.1944-9720.1996.tb01255.x

Block, D. (2014). Moving beyond "lingualism": Multilingual embodiment and multimodality in SLA. In S. May (Ed.), *The multilingual turn: Implications for SLA, TESOL, and bilingual education* (pp. 54-77). NY: Routledge.

Bremer, K. (1996). Causes of understanding problems. In K. Bremer, C. Roberts, M. Vasseur, M. Simonot, & P. Broeder (Eds.), *Achieving understanding: Discourse in intercultural encounters* (pp. 37-64). London: Longman.

Canagarajah, S. (2013). *Translingual practice: Global Englishes and cosmopolitan relations.* Abingdon, UK: Routledge.

Cogo, A. (2010). Strategic use and perceptions of English as a lingua franca. *Poznań Studies in Contemporary Linguistics, 46*, 295-312. doi:10.2478/v10010-010-0013-7

Duncan, S. (1972). Some signals and rules for taking speaking turns in conversations. *Journal of Personality and Social Psychology, 23*, 283-292. doi:10.1037/h0033031

Firth, A. (1996). The discursive accomplishment of normality: On 'lingua franca' English and conversation analysis. *Journal of Pragmatics, 26*, 237-259. doi:10.1016/0378-2166(96)00014-8

Galati, A., & Brennan, S. (2014). Speakers adapt gestures to addressees' knowledge: Implications for models of co-speech gesture. *Language, Cognition and Neuroscience, 29*, 435-451. doi:10.1080/01690965.2013.796397

Gee, J. P. (2011). *An introduction to discourse analysis: Theory and method.* London, UK: Routledge.

Giles, H., & Smith, P. (1979). Accommodation theory: Optimal levels of convergence. In H. Giles & R. Clair (Eds.), *Language and social psychology* (pp. 45-65). Oxford: Blackwell.

Goodwin, C. (2003). Pointing as situated practice. In S. Kita (Ed.), *Pointing: Where language, culture and cognition meet* (pp. 217-241). Mahwah, NJ: Lawrence Erlbaum Associates.

Gullberg, M. (1998). *Gesture as a communication strategy in second language discourse: A study of learners of French and Swedish.* Lund, Sweden: Lund University Press.

Heritage, J. (1984). A change-of-state token and aspects of its sequential placement. In J. M. Atkinson & J. Heritage (Eds.), *Structures of social action: Studies in conversation analysis* (pp. 299-345). Cambridge: Cambridge University Press.

Jefferson, G. (1984). On the organization of laughter in talk about troubles. In J. M. Atkinson & J. Heritage (Eds.), *Structures of social action: Studies in conversation analysis* (pp. 346-369). Cambridge: Cambridge University.

Jenkins, J. (2006). Current perspectives on teaching world Englishes and English as a lingua franca. *TESOL Quarterly, 40*, 157-181. doi:10.2307/40264515

Jewitt, C. (2009). An introduction to multimodality. In C. Jewitt (Ed.), *The Routledge handbook of multimodal analysis* (pp. 14-27). London: Routledge.

Kachru, B. (1996). Norms, models and identities. *The Language Teacher, 20*, 1-13. Retrieved from http://jalt-publications.org/old_tlt/files/96/oct/englishes.html

Kaur, J. (2009). *English as a lingua franca: Co-constructing understanding*. Saarbrucken: VDM Verlag.

Kaur, J. (2011). Raising explicitness through self-repair in English as a lingua franca. *Journal of Pragmatics, 43*, 2704-2715. doi:10.1016/j.pragma.2011.04.012

Ke, I., & Cahyani, H. (2014). Learning to become users of English as a lingua franca (ELF): How ELF online communication affects Taiwanese learners' beliefs of English. *System, 46*, 28-38. doi:10.1016/j.system.2014.07.008

Kendon, A. (1990). Spatial organization in social encounters: The F-formation system. In A. Kendon (Ed.), *Conducting interaction: Patterns of behaviour in focused encounters* (pp. 209-238). Cambridge: Cambridge University Press.

Kendon, A. (2004). *Gesture: Visible action as utterance*. Cambridge: Cambridge University Press.

Kita, S. (2000). How representational gestures help speaking. In. D. McNeill (Ed.), *Language and gesture* (pp. 162-185). Cambridge: Cambridge University Press.

Kress, G. (2000). Design and transformation: New theories of meaning. In B. Cope & M. Kalantzis (Eds.), *Multiliteracies: Literacy learning and the design of social futures* (pp. 153-161). London: Routledge.

Lantolf, J., & Thorne, S. (2006). *Sociocultural theory and the genesis of second language development*. New York: Oxford University Press.

Leeuwen, T. V. (2005). *Introducing social semiotics*. London: Routledge.

Matsumoto, Y. (2015). *Multimodal communicative strategies for resolving miscommunication in multilingual writing classrooms* (Unpublished doctoral dissertation). The Pennsylvania State University, Pennsylvania.

McNeill, D. (1992). *Hand and mind: What gestures reveal about thought.* Chicago, IL: University of Chicago Press.

McNeill, D. (2005). *Gesture and thought.* Chicago, IL: University of Chicago Press.

McNeill, D., & Duncan, S. D. (2000). Growth points in thinking-for-speaking. In D. McNeill (Ed.), *Language and gesture* (pp. 141-161). New York: Cambridge University Press.

Olsher, D. (2008). Gesturally-enhanced repeats in the repair turn: Communication strategy or cognitive language-learning tool? In S. G. McCafferty & G. Stam (Eds.), *Gesture: Second language acquisition and classroom research* (pp. 109-130). London: Routledge.

Sacks, H., Schegloff, E., & Jefferson, G. (1974). A simplest systematics for the organization of turn-taking for conversation. *Language, 50,* 696-735. doi:10.2307/412243

Schegloff, E. (2007). *Sequential organization in interaction: Volume 1: A primer in conversation analysis.* Cambridge: Cambridge University Press.

Seidlhofer, B. (2011). *Understanding English as a lingua franca.* Oxford: Oxford University Press.

Stam, G., & McCafferty, S. G. (2008). Gesture studies and second language acquisition: A review. In S. G. McCafferty & G. Stam (Eds.), *Gesture: Second language acquisition and classroom research* (pp. 3-24). London: Routledge.

Stein, P., & Newfield, D. (2006). Multiliteracies and multimodality in English in education in Africa: Mapping the terrain. *English Studies in Africa, 49*(1), 1-21. doi:10.1080/00138390608691341

Tuite, K. (1993). The production of gesture. *Semiotica, 93*(1-2), 83-106. doi:10.1515/semi.1993.93.1-2.83

Varonis, E. M., & Gass, S. (1985). Non-native/non-native conversations: A model for negotiation of meaning. *Applied Linguistics, 6,* 71-90. doi:10.1093/applin/6.1.71

Vasseur, M. T., Broeder, P., & Roberts, C. (1996). Managing understanding from a minority perspective. In K. Bremer, C. Roberts, M. Vasseur, M. Simonot, & P. Broeder (Eds.), *Achieving understanding: Discourse in intercultural encounters* (pp. 65-108). London: Longman.

Appendix A: Transcription Conventions
(Adapted from Jefferson 1984 and McNeill 2005)

(.)	short pause of less than 1 second
(2)	longer pause, approximate number of seconds; 2-second pauses
[	overlapping utterances
|	overlapping utterances with non-verbal actions
=	latched utterances
:	extended sound or syllable
.	fall in intonation
?	rising intonation
-	cut-off by the current speaker
°uhm°	speech much quieter than surrounding talk
Ogawamachi	emphasis
(( ))	non-verbal action
italicized words (English word)	Japanese (English translation)
→	feature of interest to analyze

編者略歴

竹田らら（たけだ　らら）　修士（文学）
現在，東京電機大学工学部英語系列講師
専門分野は，相互行為の社会言語学・大学英語における語用論教育
論文に「重複発話から創出される協調性 －親疎が異なった日本語相互行為の異ジャンル間比較からの一考察－」（単著，2016，『社会言語科学』第19巻第1号 87-102頁），「Pragmatic rules to enhance students' intercultural competence: A study based on a functional analysis of overlaps in task-based dialogues」（共著，2018，『大学英語教育学会中国・四国支部研究紀要』第15号37-54頁）など

奥切　恵（おくぎり　めぐみ）　博士（学術）
現在，聖心女子大学現代教養学部国際交流学科異文化コミュニケーションコース准教授
専門分野は，言語コミュニケーションや言語習得などの応用言語学
著書に『The acquisition of the discoursal properties of English relative constructions by Japanese learners』（2014，風間書房），『Yearbook of the German Cognitive Linguistics Association』（共著，2014，De Gruyter Mouton），『West to East, East to West: Studies in the Field of English Education』（共著，2014，成美堂）など

A Pragmatic Approach to English Language Teaching and Production

2019年12月25日　初版第1刷発行

編著者　　竹　田　ら　ら
　　　　　奥　切　　　恵

発行者　　風　間　敬　子

発行所　　株式会社　風　間　書　房
　　　〒101-0051　東京都千代田区神田神保町 1-34
　　　　電話 03(3291)5729　FAX 03(3291)5757
　　　　　　振替 00110-5-1853

印刷　太平印刷社　　製本　高地製本所

©2019　Lala Takeda　Megumi Okugiri　　NDC分類：801
ISBN978-4-7599-2309-4　　Printed in Japan
JCOPY〈(社)出版者著作権管理機構　委託出版物〉

本書の無断複製は，著作権法上での例外を除き禁じられています。複製される場合はそのつど事前に(社)出版者著作権管理機構（電話 03-5244-5088，FAX 03-5244-5089, e-mail: info@jcopy.or.jp）の許諾を得てください。